PECULIAR PETS

Rapt By Rhyme

Edited By Daisy Job

First published in Great Britain in 2021 by:

Young Writers
Remus House
Coltsfoot Drive
Peterborough
PE2 9BF
Telephone: 01733 890066
Website: www.youngwriters.co.uk

Printed and bound in the UK by BookPrintingUK
Website: www.bookprintinguk.com
YB0466CZ

★ FOREWORD ★

Welcome Reader!

Are you ready to discover weird and wonderful creatures that you'd never even dreamed of?

For Young Writers' latest competition we asked primary school pupils to create a Peculiar Pet of their own invention, and then write a poem about it! They rose to the challenge magnificently and the result is this fantastic collection full of creepy critters and amazing animals!

Here at Young Writers our aim is to encourage creativity in children and to inspire a love of the written word, so it's great to get such an amazing response, with some absolutely fantastic poems. Not only have these young authors created imaginative and inventive animals, they've also crafted wonderful poems to showcase their creations and their writing ability. These poems are brimming with inspiration. The slimiest slitherers, the creepiest crawlers and furriest friends are all brought to life in these pages – you can decide for yourself which ones you'd like as a pet!

I'd like to congratulate all the young authors in this anthology, I hope this inspires them to continue with their creative writing.

★

★ CONTENTS ★

Noah Bennett (10)	54
India Healy	56
Anais Bayne (9)	57
Bella Robbs (10)	58
Zara Berman	59
Ursula Major (11)	60
Noah Thornton	61
Luara Karl Mercer	62
Alex McKenna (9)	63
Isabelle Marsh (10)	64
Ted Keogh	65

The Willow Primary School, Tottenham

Jakub Rajek (10)	66
Sophonias Leo (10)	68
Karolina Drzewiecka (9)	70
Selena Orhan (10)	71
Israel Francis (10)	72
Joshua Duffus (10)	73
Kaia Festy (10)	74
Alex Aygun (9)	75
Natasha Anakaye Stevens (10)	76
Niah Jarmon-James (10)	77
Deniz Gulecyuz (10)	78
Kaytie Kamalanehru (10)	79
Abdullah Muhammed Dincer (10)	80
Kyra Witter-Cope (11)	81
Cinar Kacmaz (11)	82
Khepria King (11)	83
Ayan Abdul (11)	84
Esaie Mbala (9)	85
Prince Auguste (9)	86
Zaina Salah (10)	87
Sajidah Salah (9)	88
Albi Ciku (11)	89
Tim'Mia Thompson (10)	90
Aysima Guldag (10)	91
Amelia Hills (10)	92
Nadirah Nasir (9)	93
Matas Lisauskas (10)	94
Krisharn Clarke (9)	95

Phoebe Oduro-Kwarteng (10)	96
Stefania Turlea (11)	97
Hadassa Kabuiku (9)	98
Luis Ciku (9)	99
Zhir Mahdi-Outhman (9)	100
Jayden Taylor-Macauley (10)	101
Kaan Mustafa (11)	102
Selnur Sari (9)	103
Jamil Al-Abbas (10)	104
Frankie Le May (10)	105
Abigail Ochan (10)	106
Anthony Corcoran (10)	107
Ranveer Singh (10)	108
Shanaiya Theodoulou (9)	109
Zeynep Gunes (11)	110

The Winchcombe School, Shaw Estate

Effie Lunn (10)	111
Oliver Oakham (9)	112
Bethany Lloyd (10)	115
Akshara Shivakumar (9)	116
Alex Skrodzki (9)	118
James Renaut (10)	120
Emilia Muryn (10)	122
Shreeya Agarwala (9)	124
Isaac Pearton (9)	125
Alice Smith (10)	126
Rudi Frampton (10)	127
Chester Dry (10)	128
Alehandro Abdelhamed (10)	129
Amelia Newbery (10)	130
Toby Thorp (10)	131
Amelia Brunsden (10)	132
Elly Wong (10)	133
Jack Smith (10)	134
Lorri Harper (10)	135
Connor Jones (9)	136
Charlie Bortoli-Holmes (10)	137

Uphall Primary School, Ilford

Elizabeth Ikuesan (9)	138

Valence Primary School, Dagenham

Muhammad Zubair (11)	139
Ella Bailey (7)	140
Amira Ali (11)	143
Ria Day (10)	144
Faaiz (7)	145
Nina Booysen (10)	146
Maxim Hristov (7)	147
Leah Palmer (11)	148
Laura Ameny (9)	149
Isabella Hristova (7)	150
Azzam Gardaizi (11)	151
Andrei Cheaburu Maiu (7)	152
Haris Abbas (10)	153
Thomas Bampoe (11)	154
Edona Krasniqi (10)	155
Alfie Reid-Miles (10)	156
Anastasija Gurska (9)	157
Matas Tamasauskas (11)	158
Emily Nicholas (8)	159
Maria Lee (7)	160
Freddie Jones (11)	161
Megan Palmer (7)	162
Claire Angulo-Quesada (7)	163

Vicarage Primary School, East Ham

Jarrah Wajiha (10)	164
Maliha Chowdhury (10)	167
Hadiya Fahad (9)	168
Ziya Ishaq (10)	169
Jason John Selvakumar (10)	170
Kaydie Laing (11)	172

Watlington Community Primary School, Watlington

William Wedd-Johnson (8)	173
Eloise Farr (9)	174
Marley Bellamy (9)	175
Imogen Roythorne (8)	176
Jack Hansell (9)	177
Ellie Folland (8)	178
Alexi Jane Mills (9)	179
Scarlett Cuthbert (8)	180
Lara Easter (8)	181

Werrington Community Primary School, Yeolmbridge

Toby Cooper (9)	182

West Malling CE Primary School, West Malling

George Towler (11)	183
Elsie Shaw (10)	184
Millie Stevens (11)	186
Taliyah Seager (10)	188
Jessica Diamond (11)	190
Vinnie Goodayle (10)	192
Gideon Thornton (10)	193
Ava Barden (10)	194
Kian Thorn (10)	196
Joseph Trott (11)	197

Wilbraham Primary School, Fallowfield

Zunaira Osman (8)	198
Mali Aziz-Bernard (10)	200
Zuhayra Osman (10)	202
Talia Kanadil (9)	203
Nancy Mohammed (9)	204
Aaliyah Kennedy (9)	205
Minna Abdelwahab (9)	206
Aqsa (11)	207
Nur Sabier (11)	208
Nadeem Mohammed (8)	209

Faryal Nawaz Khan Naz (11)	210
Lujaynah Abubaker (10)	211
Agnieszka Jonik (10)	212
Alfie Pheasey (9)	213
Zainab Muhumad (8)	214
Sophia Rashid (8)	215
Aqsa (11)	216

Wyndcliffe Primary School, Birmingham

Resa Amin (11)	217
Eiliyah Bibi	218
Sakeenah Zafar	219
Idrees	220
Yaquub Musse Abdi (11)	221
Anaya Kayani (8)	222

Ysgol Nantgwyn, Penygraig

Lola McCarthy (9)	223
Seren Carpenter (10)	224
Jaiden Gregory (9)	225
Cole Jenkins (10)	226
Dafydd Gubbings (10)	227
Millie Phillps (9)	228
Starr Morgan-Davies (9)	229
Lynsey McCabe (10)	230
Jake Green	231

THE POEMS

Nipu

I usually see you in the morning
When the day enters through the windows

You are as soft as fluff and as light as the breeze
You are my shield against time

You are the light that makes us forget bitterness
You are the brightness that illuminates my cage

Your colours are like the mirror of the mountains
and the land

Your presence does not let loneliness know me
Your presence consoles me but it is dangerous

I'm thirsty but I want to fly high

Without saying anything, you say goodbye
I'll see you tomorrow, my dear Nipu.

Jose Maqui (11)
Prendergast Ladywell School, Lewisham

My Peculiar Pet Percy Pigeon

My pet is Percy pigeon,
He only eats a smidgen,
He doesn't turn his head right round,
He only looks both up and down,
He doesn't fly too far away,
He much prefers to come and play,
He runs around the garden just like a cat or dog,
He's often just sitting there upon the fallen log,
His most peculiar habit
Is bouncing like a rabbit,
I wouldn't change him for the world,
I love it when he's on my lap all curled.

Amelia Boyle (10)
Prendergast Ladywell School, Lewisham

Bobduck

Today, today, someone's coming to stay.
He's slimy, he's gooey and big (for his type!).
He moves around but stays in one place.
Maybe he'll come and see you one fine day.
He's loved by us all, and fun to be with.
He might be a he but he might be a she.
A friend to us all - it's a snail called Bobbi!

Olive Webb (10)
Prendergast Ladywell School, Lewisham

Monkey Nut-Munching Magpie

There is a magpie that lives outside my door,
That eats nuts we throw on the floor.
Squirrels are meant to eat them,
But the magpie always beats them.
It swoops on down,
Then circles all around.
I think this magpie is confused,
He thinks he is a monkey, which keeps me amused.

Emma Gifford-Moore (9)
Prendergast Ladywell School, Lewisham

Ready Lobster

Lucky to be a lobster,
Wouldn't it be obvious to go with a lobster to the sea,
Beautiful click noise on the street,
Some people love that mysterious beat,
Tomorrow's another day with my lobster,
Eels are his predator,
Ready, lobster?

Cosmo Atlee (9)

Prendergast Ladywell School, Lewisham

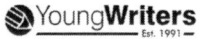

Tango The Cat

He's outside, he's inside
He'll pop up like this and he'll pop up like that
He'll scratch me sometimes if he's in a bad mood
But he is my cat Tango
And that can't compare with anything.

Dylan Famurewa (7)
Prendergast Ladywell School, Lewisham

My Pet

I care for my bear,
I love my bear's silky white hair,
He thinks ice is nice,
He knows the snow is fun,
Where he comes from he gets a lot,
You may stare at my white and fluffy polar bear!

Otis Atlee (8)

Prendergast Ladywell School, Lewisham

Pussy

P aws under claws.
U naware of cats.
S oft as cotton.
S mooth as ice.
Y awning under the couch.

Christalin Vairiah (9)

Prendergast Ladywell School, Lewisham

The Purple Turtle

I have a pet turtle
Which is an odd colour purple
Who runs like a cheetah
And no one can beat her

When people see her run
They say, "Oh, how fun!"
She runs ever so fast
That she never comes last

Who would have thought
That she'd come to a halt
And say, "I'm done!"

I love my purple turtle
Who never comes last
Because she is so fast!

Devonte Martin
South Rise Primary School, London

My Pet Cat

I have a pet cat
That sat on the mat,
He is *sooo* flat,
He once ate a bat,
That made him a cat.

Selene Olimpia Huhure (8)
South Rise Primary School, London

Racing Woods: The Peculiar Racing Dog

R acing Woods as fast as a cheetah

A nd as fast as a leopard

C hildren, watch out, Racing Woods is coming

I nsects run and hide

N eed help, Racing Woods fell over but got back up

G iants run away, Racing Woods is zooming past!

W hen I was a baby a number 1 appeared

O nly on two cheetah legs

O nly one number on him

D addies cheering for Racing Woods

S lowcoaches, hurry up.

Harry Milmer

St Andrew's CE (VA) Primary School, Fontmell Magna

The Mighty Pizard

A Pizard?
What's a pizard?
A Pizard.
Haven't you heard of a Pizard?
Of course not!
A Pizard is...
Multicoloured from head to toe
A Pizard has...
Some crazy spikes on show
A Pizard likes...
Flapping and squawking and darting and dashing
A Pizard eats...
Crunchy crackers topped with insect mashing
But what is a Pizard?
Well, if you let me explain...
A Pizard is coloured red, green and blue
If you think that's cool, you should see its poo!
A Pizard has scales that shine bright in the sun
And feathers that flutter magnificently when it
shakes its bum!

Wow! A Pizard sounds cool! *But what is it?*
Pizard, Mizard, Fizard, Gizard...
If you don't know by now, you don't know a Pizard!

Charlie Richardson (8)

St Andrew's CE (VA) Primary School, Fontmell Magna

Chimara!

Chimara lives on a fiery plain,
The ground is always burning,
He likes to roam and sun his mane,
To relax he rolls in the mud, turning.

His best friend is his owner,
Who goes by the name of Jonathan.
He plays all day and rolls in the hay,
Hiding from their enemy
Soloman.

He eats fire for breakfast, birds for lunch,
And spicy goats after that,
But his favourite meal he'll climb over hills for,
Is a nice big pepperoni pizza-shaped hat.

He'll travel with his friend,
Travelling in vortexes of mirrored worlds,
Where opposites are without end,
And the winds always whirl,
And the heat ebbs away,
By the light of the day

Forever and ever,
They hunt... for the diamond lever.

Jonathan Hughes (8)
St Andrew's CE (VA) Primary School, Fontmell Magna

Tom Bamboo

My friend is a skateboarding panda
His name is Tom Bamboo
He goes to the park on Saturdays
He tells me to come along too

He goes fast on his skateboard
While I just walk along
Tom Bamboo does tricks *aallll* day
While he listens to bamboo songs

He can front flip, backflip and kick flip great
And drops in on ramps that are steep
He said he'll teach me a backflip one day
But for now, he needs to sleep.

Sagen Francis (8)
St Andrew's CE (VA) Primary School, Fontmell Magna

Eclipse

Eclipse is a peculiar dragon,
Whose scales are shiny and black,
She loves to ride a wagon,
Because there's lots of room at the back.

Eclipse is a night light dragon,
Whoo breathes out fumes of fire,
She's friends with a Crocaroo called Alan,
But she can fly much higher.

Eclipse is so extraordinary,
She can glow in the dark, you see
Making the dark seem ordinary
Lighting the way for you and me.

Tilly Childs (8)
St Andrew's CE (VA) Primary School, Fontmell Magna

Speedy Tortoise

There once was a speedy tortoise
Who made his shell very moist
He was very fast
In any race, he would not come last
He was a part of the particular pets crew
If he was running he would run straight past you
Now I come to an end to my song
If you listen carefully you can hear his winning bells
going *dong!*

Emma Oakley

St Andrew's CE (VA) Primary School, Fontmell Magna

Rory The Rapping Rhino

There's a rhino called Rory,
And this is his story,
As a rhino he is strong,
But he sings his own song,
He always raps,
And he never takes naps,
His friends think he is cool,
Because he makes his own rules,
He's the best rapping rhino you will ever see,
One day you might see him on TV!

Zach Pickford (8)

St Andrew's CE (VA) Primary School, Fontmell Magna

Betsy's Wish

B etsy the terrific turtle is the fastest on the beach

E ating delicious seaweed and gobbling jellyfish

T rying to swim in the big blue bay was Betsy's only wish

S he ran too fast and started to soar way up in the air

Y ou can do whatever you put your mind to, just like Betsy!

Aphra Pinder (8)

St Andrew's CE (VA) Primary School, Fontmell Magna

Flying Pandas

Soaring, swooping in the sky
Elegantly descending to the ground
Munching, chewing on bamboo shrubs
In the jungle what do you see?
Bright coloured flowers, red, orange and yellow
Darting into the sky
Gaining speed, taking off to the sky
Fly high, fly high with me.

Nazna Thom (8)
St Andrew's CE (VA) Primary School, Fontmell Magna

Wrecker

Wrecker makes a wrecking sound.
He uses his head to pound and pound.
He enjoys to destroy,
Don't mistake him for a toy.
A ball for a head and a crane for a tail
And he's bigger than a whale.

William Samways (8)

St Andrew's CE (VA) Primary School, Fontmell Magna

Silly Smash

I found a flying snake
Flying high above the lake
He flew down on my head
So I took him home to go to bed
I called him Silly Smash
Now he likes eating the smelly trash!

Ellie-Mae Ayres (8)

St Andrew's CE (VA) Primary School, Fontmell Magna

My Pet

My friend is called Emma, the first rainbow-winged, flying unicorn dog in the world.
She can jump as high as the tallest man and has the biggest ears to hear me when I call her from a mile away
She has the largest rainbow wings that can make her fly over the biggest mountains and the largest oceans to be there for me.
Her sparkly horn that glitters in the dark keeps me feeling safe all night through.
She is very friendly and kind, she loves me very much.
She licks my face and curls up by my side at night to keep me warm and safe.
I love Emma and Emma loves me
She is a very special dog but even more special to me.

Autumn Hadley (8)

St Gerard's RC Primary School, Castle Vale

Molly The Magnificent Magnetic Cat

Molly is a magnificent cat, there is absolutely no doubt about that!
Her paws stick to the metal doors
Her magnetic claws deserve a round of applause
She is a fun and happy cat
Even though she sticks to the mat
Her powers are special and we all have that feeling
Especially when she walks on the ceiling
She ate some magnets a long time ago
Now she is magnetic and goes with the flow
I love my Molly, she is cuddly and cute
She can even play a tune on the flute.

Sebastian Codner (8)

St Gerard's RC Primary School, Castle Vale

Terrific Tiger Family

T ame, terrific tiger scavenging in the zoo
E ager elephant following too
R oaring and snoring as crawling begins
R udley rushing past other animals
I nterrogating tiger yawns loudly
F amilies of animals heading to bed
I ntelligent elephants splashing water
C urious caterpillars crawling around.

Sahel Soltan (8)

St Gerard's RC Primary School, Castle Vale

Fashion Flamingo

A fashion flamingo, tall and fine,
With her hat and heels, pink and lime,
She lived in a village, small and smelly.
She could not stand it, she cried mentally,
She had lots of jewels, ruby and red,
"But what could I do with them?" she sadly said.
But then one day a little frog said,
"If you don't give me your jewels I'll cut off your head."
"Oh no, oh no," she cried with sorrow.
"I can't give you my jewels, I'll give you them tomorrow."
"No, no, no, you'll give me them now, not tomorrow."
Fashion Flamingo swung her leg up high all the way into the sky,
And kicked the frog way up high,
She happily, joyfully danced with joy,
And she sighed with laughter while dancing with joy.

Olivia Carberry (10)
St Oswald's CE Primary School, Bootle

Timmy The Turtle

In the middle of the night
When there is nobody in sight
The little eggs hatch
And a new life has just begun

A little turtle named Timmy
He gives lots of things like happiness to me
He reaches the ocean he goes in
One year later of wandering the ocean he goes to
have an adventure

He reaches for a fruit in a tree
Suddenly, he looks and sees a bee
He becomes very happy
With some company

The rocks smash
They crash all the branches
We better run or we're done!

We get out safely, get in an abandoned boat
In the end, I made a new friend
And our friendship will never break or bend

Now we have a new place to call home

We enjoy living in the boat, searching and discovering new adventures.

Laís Gouveia (10)
St Oswald's CE Primary School, Bootle

A Day In The Life Of A Peculiar Porse!

Long ago there lived a creature called a peculiar
porse
A peculiar porse was a mix of a horse
His name is Pog because he is a pig as well
He looked in the mirror and saw his teeth were
yellow but he was quite mellow!
He got his white toothpaste and brushed his teeth
that turned pearly white
He went downstairs and wiggled his piggy tail that
is pink
He went outside and was not surprised!
His parents had bought him another Porsche
because he is a peculiar porse
He went to the other porses and said, "Hello,
matey mellow!"
He drove home in his new Porsche and had so
much fun!
But sorry folks this poem is nearly done but stay
for tomorrow because this has been fun!

Esme Hughes (10)
St Oswald's CE Primary School, Bootle

The Flying Superhero Doggo

The very cute dog AKA Flying Dog Master the
superhero with a cape on its back
A collar like tape, it's massive!
Got pace like a mouse but too mad in a house

Whenever he gets food he's grumpy and hungry
He gets a little bumpy when he's finished though

He jumps like mad with his cape bouncing
Then he jumps into his cage like nothing happened
He's not an ordinary dog but better if we put him
in a net
But if he falls out, he's going to the vet.

Alfie Maguire (9)
St Oswald's CE Primary School, Bootle

The Shog

Long ago there was a creature called a shog
It looked like a snake and a dog
Its tail was scaly and his legs were plumpy
And when he ate his tea he sure was grumpy

By a town in a forest
He lived near in a bush
Waiting for prey to come in touch
When he had a snack his teeth went *crunch crunch*

Sometimes he was tired and he stretched
And slithered to his lair
And closed his eyes
Walked in a circle and went to sleep.

Mikey Radford (10)
St Oswald's CE Primary School, Bootle

The Multi-Powered Lobyhogy

Lobyhogy wants some fun
Five more minutes till break but he does not like
this sum

Five minutes pass
He wants to know because he's so fast

Ninja Cat challenges him
So they race, how fast he is
Ninja Cat stops and says,
"How fast, he starts with a blast."

He teleports back
And says, "Too hot for you to handle."
And flies back to his castle.

Josh Ponting (10)
St Oswald's CE Primary School, Bootle

Sling The Extraordinary

Sling the dog
Who is rather quite ordinary
But when it hits 12pm
He becomes very extraordinary

Fighting criminals through the night
They can't even see him in plain sight
Pow! Whizz! Bang! he goes
Flying through the night
When the night fades away
And the sun appears over the dark, dismal city
Sling flies over to his house for some rest.

Nathan Grocott (9)
St Oswald's CE Primary School, Bootle

The Dragon Dog

My dog Axel is very smart
As well with his kind heart
When I am down he changes my frown

The sky is lovely and blue
Like his scales are too
He breathes red and yellow fire
And leaves a sapphire trail

He can fly high in the sky
And is very tall but cannot be small
He is the best dragon dog you can see
But he is still working on his training.

Layton Sole (10)
St Oswald's CE Primary School, Bootle

Midnight

Midnight sweeps around the town, covering the
light of the sky,
A bat named Midnight also flies and hears the
sleeping children,
But one child stays awake and watches the bat fly,
And Midnight comes down from the roof to say hi,
Midnight curls up in the child's hands,
And Midnight the bat falls asleep feeling quite
grand!

Eve Reardon (10)
St Oswald's CE Primary School, Bootle

Spider-Man Spider...

In the dead of night, my pet will fight
And kick butts if it's needed
If he gets wet he'll go back to his web
And wake up lots in the evening
His kindness will break and turn into anger or hate
And he will go proper evil
And become a villain of the evening.

Max Adams (9)
St Oswald's CE Primary School, Bootle

My Dog Stan

My dog Stan sits around, jumps around, the best he can.
He likes a tickle, he likes a hug and sleeps on his rug.
Stan's named after Grandad, who thought it was an odd name.
But that's what Mum called him just the same.
Love sausages, bacon and treats and loves going to the beach.

Alex Carr (10)
St Oswald's CE Primary School, Bootle

Ninja Cat

My cat Milo acts like a ninja
He's not a winger
And karate chops dogs in the face
Then hops on his motorbike and speeds away at pace
Sees another opponent
And karate kicks him in the face.

Zack Dutton (9)
St Oswald's CE Primary School, Bootle

My Great Giraffe

My great giraffe followed me to the
Half park, half circus.
People were gathering for a great show.
Me and my giraffe were getting ready backstage.
The staff came into the room to help us with
getting ready.
When it was time for the show, me and my great
giraffe stood behind the curtains.
The curtains opened.
The show began.
At first, Giraffe was very confused.
Everyone was staring right at us like they were evil
eagles.
But my great giraffe understood with a nod and
jumped onto the highest rope on the stage!
People cheered but with fear.
My great giraffe jumped off the rope line and
dragged out a unicycle!
He started riding on it.
The crowd cheered.
The giraffe and the staff smiled.
Employing my annoying great giraffe friend is
great!

Joshua Vuvu Mantumbu
St Sebastian's RC Primary School, Douglas Green

Jack The Lazy Crocodile

Jack the lazy crocodile likes sleeping in a river
He swishes his head here and he swishes his head there
He swishes his head when people come and disturb him
So don't you dare get a stick to poke him.
He's a mean little crocodile, no one likes him that are in the river
Not even the little fishes like him because he lets the fishes come and eats them all up.
The poor little fishes do not know where to go
Wherever they go he catches up, they are so scared to death.
They're so scared about getting eaten! Argh!
The crocodile eats them all up so sad, the poor little fishes.

Lydia Ye (7)
St Sebastian's RC Primary School, Douglas Green

A Peculiar Pet

I have a pet,
That many don't have.
I would call him Dave,
But it doesn't sound brave.

His tail, which is surely long,
Could knock you out
With a simple
Bing, bang, bong!

His snapping jaws,
With many conical teeth,
Continuously gnaw
On those poor old paws!

His four short legs,
With those dear webbed toes,
Push him around
In the fast-flowing water.

If you haven't realised by now,
I'll give you a hint
That you will appreciate!

They are regularly green in skin or brown,
And they have a V-shaped snout!
They also have a close relative.
They are blackish-grey
And have a U-shaped snout!

Cherie Liu (10)

St Sebastian's RC Primary School, Douglas Green

Terry The Tortoise

Terry the tortoise is my companion.
He once lived at the Grand Canyon.
One day he grew old,
He just couldn't keep out the cold.

Step by step, he reached the cage.
How long did it take? Three. Whole. Days.
Gradually, he became nimble,
Suddenly, it became a symbol
Of strength, speed and power.

He had to show his owner.
Zoom!
What was that flash?
Little did they know a tortoise just dashed...

Saleisha Sithole (11)
St Sebastian's RC Primary School, Douglas Green

Toby's Magic Antlers

Toby the deer
Was full of cheer
His antlers were magical
His life was radical
Toby's antlers shimmered
His magic was delivered
He loved to tap dance
And floated off to France
He flew up the Eiffel Tower
And gave everyone a superpower
Toby was amazed
Everyone praised
He flew off to space
Like he was in a race
He landed on Mars
Where he gazed at the stars.

Sophie Allan (9)
St Sebastian's RC Primary School, Douglas Green

Minobeous

This is a strange story of an even stranger creature
called the Minobeous,
It could turn into anything but it could not do
anything else,
One cold and chilly night a boy went looking for
the Minobeous,
When he found it he got a funny feeling in his
tummy,
Because he had heard strange rumours about
what the Minobeous looked like,
But it looked nothing like what people had said.

It looked like a blob sort of thing floating around,
He saw shapes in it but the shapes never stayed
still and they were always moving,
It did have colour though, at the moment it was
blue, very light blue.

So the boy came close, hand on sword,
Then he realised that the Minobeous was lying
down and was not moving,
So he got out his net and suddenly the Minobeous
became a light blue hedgehog,

However, the boy was startled. Why had that happened?
He swiped at the Minobeous (the hedgehog) and said, "I am taking you home."

And so the boy did take the Minobeous home,
Though he was yet to find out about it and what it could do,
On the way home the Minobeous (Minob for short) became a blob again,
But it was a different colour this time, it was a colour that would be described as very scared.

The boy had not realised this so he kept on walking.
A while later the boy and the Minobeous saw another strange creature,
The boy had heard about them, they were dark whispers,
A strange creature that had long thin tails with feelers on the edge and
Bodies with arms that appeared to be webbed to their body,
Their feelers would wrap around your head and make it feel like you were in your happiest dream,

However, they would also drain the energy from you until you dropped dead.

The Minobeous knew that they would be able to completely drain him,
So he tried to escape and attempted to turn into a dark whisper,
But he could not because a dark whisper is something dreadful,
It is one's soul torn from a body and all that is left is grief, anger, sadness, regret and envy.

But most importantly greed, once you have turned over to the dark side you can never truly become pure,
Because once you turn over to the dark side you have simply let your bad side take over,
The good side, however, simply wants balance,
So it can never take over even if someone was always happy,
That simply means it is even harder to become fully good there is,

So what I want you to think about is how they survived the dark whisper because no one knows how.
All we know is that when they emerged from the forest there were two people as one.

Harvey Conlon (9)
Stanford Junior School, Brighton

Peculiar Pets

There's so little you know about a pet,
And so I'd advise you not to forget,
That when you're sleeping or out and about,
They say, "Party time!" and that I don't doubt.

Now where to start?
How about mice?
They worship and play computer games,
Like they're some holy device.

The French bulldog
Is an excellent chef,
But that is amazing,
As he is quite deaf.

As for the tortoises,
This I must say,
They dress up as monsters,
And scare people all day!

Over to the budgies,
They give everyone a shock,

As their owner's voice
They perfectly mock.

The cheeky poodle,
Begs and pretends to be poor,
When it has enough money,
It runs away out the door.

The kittens dress up,
And hang up a glitter ball,
They shout, "Time to *dance!*
However big, however small!"

The multiple lizards
Are the DJs of the day and night,
They lead the fiasco,
It is such a delight!

The jangling of keys
Is the next noise they hear,
The owner could have heard them,
The air fills with fear.

They quickly pack up,
As fast as they could,

Before they are told,
They are up to no good.

Then the door opens,
And the owner walks in,
"Hello, all of you!
How good have you been?"

Mia Coates (9)
Stanford Junior School, Brighton

The Everlasting Phoenix

As she is reborn from the ashes she spreads her
wings up to the sky
The everlasting phoenix will take you by surprise
Feathers bright like flames
Beak as sharp as a knife
The everlasting phoenix will burn again tonight
As she soars across the midnight sky
Floating on the wind
She feels free at last like she will always win
Wings as wide as the eye can see
Eyes as deep as a single dream
When she flies she is never seen
Just in her own world, being free
When she reaches her abandoned cave
She's had enough of being brave
She lies down again once more
And burns right down, not frightening at all.

Maia Revill (10)
Stanford Junior School, Brighton

What Am I?

I'm sparkly and glittery,
I take baths in rainbows,
And I love lollipops,
Who am I?
What am I?

I fly high across the sky,
Higher than any bird could reach,
Making people's days as I go by,
Who am I?
What am I?

I love to spread joy around the world,
And love making people happy,
I'm mystical, I'm magical,
Who am I?
What am I?

It's clear as day,
Black as night,
Surely you don't want more clues?

I spread rainbows and glitter wherever I go,
I'm a sucker for sugar,
And I make the sun shine at day,
And I make the stars twinkle at night,

I'm a unicorn,
I'm mystical,
I'm magical,
And I'm free as can be.

Noah Bennett (10)
Stanford Junior School, Brighton

The Tiger

The tiger is independent, living on his own, roaming
his territory,
His eyes scanning the jungle for food, looking in
the leaves
His ears, sharp, pointy, pricked, listening for the
slightest sound
His stripes, misplaced, dark, black, like death
peering into the body
His claws scratching the ground, ready to pounce
into the air as though he was flying
His nose could smell you even if he was blind in a
room with perfume
His tail swaying in the wind like a kite
His whiskers, sensitive, spiky, keeping his face safe
from tight spaces
He shall never be extinct
Because he is my pet.

India Healy
Stanford Junior School, Brighton

Meet Bailey

A black beauty
His fur as dark as coal in the night sky
But his soul shines as bright as the brightest star
He wags his tail as fast as the speed of light
A gentle giant slowly walking to his bed
As fluffy as a cotton cloud in a dream world
And claws as sharp as lions' teeth
His eyes are as pretty as a diamond
His teeth gnashing with food
This is my dog!

Anais Bayne (9)
Stanford Junior School, Brighton

Ted The Dog

Once upon a time, there was a dog called Ted,
He loved to stretch his body on my big double bed,
And Ted liked a strange thing, guess what he liked to do
He liked to go surfing on my loo
I would play with him in the rain,
My mum and dad would watch from the windowpane
When I gave him his food,
I'd set him in the mood,
To watch a movie with more food.

Bella Robbs (10)
Stanford Junior School, Brighton

What Am I?

Jumping around the cage like popcorn in a pan,
In search of their favourite treat.
Alert and ready, their ruby-red shiny eyes look into
the outside world.
They emerge blending into each other,
Different shades of caramel, liquorice and white.
Their talon-feet prance around as if on stage like
stompy ballerinas.

Zara Berman
Stanford Junior School, Brighton

Okapi

I am an okapi, the unknown, forest giraffe
Striped legs that make me invisible between the
waving leaves.
I am an okapi, king of the jungle without a mane.
Miniature horns that act like tiny shields.
Crash go the horns fighting for a hornless okapi.
I am an okapi.

Ursula Major (11)
Stanford Junior School, Brighton

Anger

Anger is a dog
He is red
His soul looks like a burning building that will never
burn out
His scent smells like smoke from a raging fire
His breath tastes like revenge
His howl sounds like claws on a chalkboard
His fur feels like a ragged cliff.

Noah Thornton
Stanford Junior School, Brighton

Lowland Streaked Tenrec

Lowland streaked tenrec
The tenrec is as small as a rat
It eats earthworms
It is black and yellow
Its nose is long
Predators are people and mongeese
It lives in Madagascar's lowlands
There are lots of unknown animals to unlock.

Luara Karl Mercer
Stanford Junior School, Brighton

The Puffin Pig

I move like a chicken with wings
I have a beak as hard as stone, claws like needles
When it is as dark as a cave
And there is not a single sound
I toddle out to eat fresh food upon the cliff edge
And gaze at the stars in the sky.

Alex McKenna (9)
Stanford Junior School, Brighton

The Fennec Fox

Solemn, young and fascinating
Dark, piercing eyes
Nose, small and black
Ears, tall and high
Legs, bold and thin
Tail, luscious and long
All the things a fox could wish for.

Isabelle Marsh (10)
Stanford Junior School, Brighton

Fred

I remember little Fred
Who was my hamster.
Now he's dead.
He used to climb all around
Looking for honey sticks
On the ground.

Ted Keogh
Stanford Junior School, Brighton

Jack And The Mean Hawk

Jack is a cute, furry, chubby cat.
He likes to sit on a red mat.
When Jack gets hit, he jumps and says: "Stop!"
All Jack does is eat and listen to pop.

One day, he went for a big walk.
The weather was good and suddenly he saw a
hawk.
"Hey, cat, do you want magic milk?
You can fly like me. Think!
All that I want is a piece of cheese.
Bring me cheese from your house, please."
Jack thought for a moment and ran to his house.
"When I will fly, I will catch that annoying mouse!"

He came back with a big piece of cheese.
The hawk, gave him gold, round keys.
"Use these to open this green garden door
Then you will find magic milk on the floor."

Jack took the keys and found a green door
But he couldn't find the magic milk on the floor.

All that he heard was a hawk laugh.
"You are so silly cat, ha ha ha!"

Jakub Rajek (10)
The Willow Primary School, Tottenham

Crazy Carl

Crazy Carl's an insane cat,
His favourite meal is boiled bat.
Crazy Carl's a bursting bubble of food,
You can't talk to him because he is the definition of rude.
Crazy Carl plays an electric guitar,
He's always utterly broke 'cause he smashes his car.

Crazy Carl constantly dies,
He always has in mind that he has nine lives.
Crazy Carl has massive blue eyes,
Maybe it's 'cause he has a secret disguise.
Crazy Carl terrifies all the dogs,
I don't know why but he can't scare frogs.

Crazy Carl's a giant ball of badness,
But when his mum's around he reeks at showing kindness.
Crazy Carl thinks he's cool,
But when he sleeps he starts to drool.

Crazy Carl has pet ants,
When he can't find them they're down his underpants.

Bored Carl has had enough of being crazy,
Now his full-time job is being lazy.

Sophonias Leo (10)

The Willow Primary School, Tottenham

The Hilarious Hippo

H ilarious Hippo is a very unusual hippo.

I t is honestly a hippo who is smart and loves art,

L ike he would even be able to paint you!

A nd he ain't gonna faint, phew!

R ight, let's get this straight. He

I s a little overweight but that's okay for him.

"O h, wow!" everyone says when they see him because

U s people, you know, are normal but Hippo is not.

S uper Hippo he calls himself but it's more like Scooper Hippo.

H ippo has always loved his lovely, ugly sister, she

I s a little crazy, lazy hippo but that's what he loves her for.

P oppy Hippo is her name but he calls her Floppy Hippo just to make her annoyed.

P hew! Great that Hippo has got a helmet. If not, he would be finished.

O h, I never knew that Hippo was a super hilarious hippo!

Karolina Drzewiecka (9)

The Willow Primary School, Tottenham

My Cat Is A Superhero Cat!

Did you know what I recently found out?
My cat is in fact a superhero cat!
It was then when I stumbled in the kitchen in the middle of the night
When I noticed creepy shadows flying around!
They were making haunting sounds, sending shivers to my hands.
And then I screamed for help, saying: "Help, they found me out!"
Suddenly, like a thunder light, I saw my cat, flying through the shadows, like a fire knight.
I couldn't believe my eyes when he was fighting with all he had.
Shooting blue flames which extinguished darkness like mad!
And then, there was silence and peace
I was very happy and glad.
From now on, whilst I am living my daily life
I and my cat are the best shadows fighters this world has ever had.

Selena Orhan (10)

The Willow Primary School, Tottenham

Wally The Wolf

Hi, my name's Wally,
I am the wolf's owner and I will tell you all about
Wally the wolf.

He has grey fur, white paws and red eyes. He can
see so far, he sees all over the land.

Wally is the protector of his lands, he loves eating
meat and he has powers.
I will tell you all about it...
He can fly, shape-shift, has laser eyes, can teleport,
has speed and mega-strength.
He is always there to save the day.

"Oh no, there's a robber!" you cry.
Wally the wolf comes to save us. "Wow, he is
fighting them!"
"Yay! He beat them! Time to go to jail, robbers!"
"Ha ha ha ha!" and now it's time to go home and
celebrate Wally.

Israel Francis (10)
The Willow Primary School, Tottenham

Unisaurous

Under the canopy of green leaves, a sight of
wonder lies within
Nobody dares go but if someone does
Inside the terrifying monster will fill up like lava
inside
Shimmering eyes like stars and how it gracefully
flies in the moonlit sky
Anyone who sees its razor-sharp like teeth may not
live another day on that mountain
Many try to spot the mysterious creature but none
have succeeded
Remember, there is danger and beauty to be seen

In the beauty of the mountains, I behold a sight of
wonder
The colourful wings of a creature unknown
The shriek of its warning call sends shivers down
my spine
The breath of fire has me frozen on the spot
Its eyes that pierce into your soul.

Joshua Duffus (10)
The Willow Primary School, Tottenham

My Bird Tincle Tims

T inkle tinkle go the bells at the end of my bird's little tail,

I n my hands so soft, so light, as his feathers shine so bright,

N ests are his home where he silently rests,

C ome and see his rainbow coat while we float on my boat,

L earn the ways of his peaceful song that he sings so quietly,

E very tweet that he squeaks sounds so nice and sweet.

T he way you soar and sweep the skies stops the world in fascination,

I nteresting is your big, long, bent beak that glistens in the dark,

M ost beautiful things are your light red wings,

S o softly you speak, yet you don't say a word.

Kaia Festy (10)
The Willow Primary School, Tottenham

My Dog Danny

My dog Danny is full of love and soft as a dove.
He has a black nose.
With me, he's very close.

My dog Danny is full of joy and
His teddy is his favourite toy.
He never barks at any dog.
He only goes and bites a log.

My dog Danny loves to play,
Especially when it's a hot day.
He loves when I rub his tummy,
He always thinks it's funny.

My dog Danny is fluffy and shiny,
But his ears look tiny.
His eyes are as big as the moon,
And he sleeps until noon.

My dog Danny runs and spins,
Just because he wants to win.
He goes crazy when he sees meat,
He is first to come and eat.

Alex Aygun (9)
The Willow Primary School, Tottenham

My Terrific Tiger

My terrific tiger is the prettiest of them all.
My terrific tiger is the fastest of them all.
We always go on trips,
But we never need any tips,
Because my terrific tiger is the smartest of them all.

My terrific tiger is as fast as a car.
My terrific tiger is the strongest by far.
We will never be separated,
If we did, I know I'd hate it.
Because my terrific tiger behaves the best by far.

My terrific tiger has orange and white stripes,
My terrific tiger has soft fur. He never bites!
He can't fly into the sky,
But I love him - you know why?
Because my terrific tiger is the best in all the sites.

Natasha Anakaye Stevens (10)
The Willow Primary School, Tottenham

Cattycorn

C attycorn is a stupendous cat.

A t the park, she shows off her uncanny skills on a mottled mat.

T here are multiple tricks she can do.

T hese are some of them, maybe you would like them too!

Y oga, splits, magic and massages. She has also won a painting competition.

C attycorn is a friend of everyone and it all started at a 3,000 person exhibition.

O liver Kit is her best friend and everyone says he's just one of the best cats in the world.

R eally they are clever clogs, but today they were curled-up kittens.

N ow no one knew where they had put their old-fashioned sleeping mittens...

Niah Jarmon-James (10)
The Willow Primary School, Tottenham

Bunnytastic!

B unnytastic is a very iconic pet

U nique as a pop star and as cuddly as a teddy bear she is

N othing will stop her from being this cute

N one of the other bunnies in the world are as cute as Bunnytastic

Y our eyes will turn into hearts when you look into her bright blue eyes

T he most vulnerable thing in the world is Bunnytastic

A s cute and iconic as she is aggressive

S o watch out!

T rendy, sassy and beautiful are just only three words to describe Bunnytastic

I f she comes next to you you will see a ball of bright pink cotton candy

C an you resist this cuteness?

Deniz Gulecyuz (10)
The Willow Primary School, Tottenham

Corrupted Fox

C ourageous is one of the words to describe it

O ne of a kind it is!

R oar! That is the sound of it at night

R eckless and sly

U nique and different from other foxes

P oor and restless but always villainous

T his special pet will be mine and only mine

E yes red like blood and always looking into trouble

D ark like the midnight sky

F luffy but scary with black lightning-like tears underneath its eyes

O nce you look into its eyes you could never unsee it again

X -rays of this creature show that it is different from the others.

Kaytie Kamalanehru (10)

The Willow Primary School, Tottenham

Invinsacroc

I n the forest lived a crocodile

N ow now, don't be scared when we say crocodile

V ampires are scarier if you ask me

I nvinsacroc has the power of invisibility

N ever challenge him to a game of hide-and-seek

S lowly he will sneak and grab you by the cheek

A pples are his favourite fruit

C runch, crunch, he eats away all day from the root

R hino is the only one who understands him

O h, how they both love to swim

C ome along now, don't be scared, Crocs could be your new best friend.

Abdullah Muhammed Dincer (10)

The Willow Primary School, Tottenham

Electric Ellie

As night pours upon the winter air, gold lightning
bolts glisten with fear
Tonight is the time to strike with power and not to
be as sweet as a blooming flower
Courageous, she zooms into the midnight skies,
searching for a battle as she flies
Her grey, soft fur ruffles against the leaves, past
the bare trees
Her eyes shimmer like twinkling stars
Her shadow stands proud in the moonlit sky
This peculiar pet is one of a kind, so special, so
sweet, so powerful, is what she sees
Her name is Ellie and she soars in the sky.
Electric Ellie is a lightning bolt of pride!

Kyra Witter-Cope (11)
The Willow Primary School, Tottenham

Strengtho

Stronger than a lion
Will be there when you're dying
He is a strong dog
He has muscles thicker than a log
'The name's Strengtho' is his most attractive line
His favourite number is number nine

He has perfect eyesight
Even when there's moonlight
Strengtho runs faster than a cheetah
Has white fur like an akita
He hates cats
And he has enemies like bats

He loves to share food
Especially with his dudes
He has a red eye
And a friend that could fly
He is brave
And he lives in a cage.

Cinar Kacmaz (11)
The Willow Primary School, Tottenham

Bonny The Cannon-Blasting Cat!

There he is! There he is! It's Bonny the cannon-blasting cat!
All of the crowd is cheering as he puts on his tiny, shiny hat!

This is so exciting, Bonny has climbed into the cannon,
My legs are wobbling more than a giraffe balancing on a salmon.

Whoosh! Wow! Bonny has been blasted into the air! Just look at him soaring,
Nobody can say that Bonny the cannon-blasting cat is boring!

I'm allowed to get an autograph from Bonny later, I can't wait to see him!
Maybe when I'm older, I can even be him!

Khepria King (11)
The Willow Primary School, Tottenham

Ferocious Falcon Fox

F erocious Falcon Fox can fly very high

A ll the way past the trees and to the sky

L ettuce my ferocious Falcon Fox loves oh so much!

C lever Falcon Fox uses her agility to cheekily steal it from our lunch

O ver the table across to our plates

N aughty Falcon Fox, how much lettuce she would take!

F alcon Fox, oh how she soars!

O ver towers and through the clouds she tore!

X -ray fish she also loves, she can scoff two in a second or even more!

Ayan Abdul (11)

The Willow Primary School, Tottenham

Douglas The Dog

My pet is a superhero who can fly and teleport.
His name is Douglas.
The adventures Douglas and I have been on are:
Rock climbing,
Scuba diving and even more.
Too many to mention!

My pet is determined, kind, strong and even
talented.
He can do a lot of cool stuff like back-flips, front-
flips and backhand springs.
My pet has even joined a band!
I have trained him so hard,
He can do better things in his life than any pooch.
He wants to become the most popular dog in the
world.

Esaie Mbala (9)
The Willow Primary School, Tottenham

Jaunty Jaguar

Jaunty Jaguar was not like any ordinary jaguar,
He was kind and helpful.
Everyone loved him!
He would buy the best outfits,
He was really fashionable.
He could talk and fly and he was the best
superhero in the world!

One beautiful day, Pleasant Pig showed up at his
house and asked to find out who was the best
superhero.
Jaunty Jaguar agreed.
The challenge began!
Jaguar saved Bear, Sheep, and Cow,
While Pig only saved Lion.
Jaguar won!
We were all cheering (even Pig).

Prince Auguste (9)
The Willow Primary School, Tottenham

The Powerful Catfressor

When you're in danger,
Do not fear,
Do you want to know why?
The Powerful Catfressor is here.

He doesn't have scales,
Or razor-sharp claws,
So don't be terrified,
He is cute and has soft paws.

Zoom! He goes past you,
This cat is extraordinary,
Catfressor always has a victory,
But he is not ordinary.

So next time,
You see this heroic superhero,
Don't say he is nothing,
Because Catfressor is not zero.

Zaina Salah (10)
The Willow Primary School, Tottenham

The Magnificent Mia

When you are in an emergency,
Do not fear,
Just stay calm and stay where you are,
Because Magnificent Mia will be near.

Don't think she's scary,
She's very glary,
She's very soft and furry,
Sometimes she can be purry,

Magnificent Mia is the best,
Don't worry,
She can pass any hard test,
In a hurry.

She is fantastic,
She is marvellous at gymnastics,
She is fast as lightning,
She is the best at fighting.

Sajidah Salah (9)
The Willow Primary School, Tottenham

The Villain Husky

There was a villain in a flash.
He does a slash with his poison claws.
His jaws are poisonous.
He is the one and only villain that can match the superhero.
He is the best villain in the world.
He can lift a car with his finger without a sweat.
Running around looking for mischief.
He gets what he is looking for.
Knocking everyone out without a sweat.
He can do whatever he wants.
No one can stop him.
He is the definition of strong.

Albi Ciku (11)

The Willow Primary School, Tottenham

Siennagames

Sienna is not a normal dog.
She is a dog that no one has ever seen before.
She is the type of dog to play video games.
So I gave her the name Siennagames.
Plus she is very good at it, maybe better than you.

The games she mostly plays are Fortnite and Minecraft
And she has won lots of cups.
Therefore, once we counted the money that she got
And it was 22 million overall
And then we were rich and started making YouTube videos.

Tim'Mia Thompson (10)
The Willow Primary School, Tottenham

The Life Of Spotty The Cow

S   potty the cow is her name,
P   eople always love stroking her,
O   h, you're probably wondering who strokes a
    cow,
T   his cow has the softest fur,
T   he fur has big black spots,
Y   es, it is all over her body.

C   ows love hay but Spotty the cow loves...
O   atmeal with strawberries.
W   ell, she won't eat it if it doesn't have mini
    marshmallows.

Aysima Guldag (10)
The Willow Primary School, Tottenham

The Circus Hare

The hare loved to be in the air
The crowd went *woohoo* as she flew across the trapeze
She loved to eat cheese
Her tail was a fluffy blanket
Her ears were gigantic
Her teeth were one metre long
She was in the circus all day long

Her fur was short and warm
And she hated it when there was a rainstorm
She loved the circus
When she was on the trapeze that is what she would focus on.

Amelia Hills (10)
The Willow Primary School, Tottenham

Passionate Phoenix

I took my passionate phoenix outside for some
fresh air and
Whoosh! Whoosh!
His horns were as thick as trees and
His eyes were as red as rubies.
Flying high in the rosy sky,
Running into marshmallow clouds.
Passing polite, graceful birds...
Uh-oh!
We were about to crash into a plane!
His ruby eyes saw and whooshed away,
Bringing us back home.
Phew! That was close!

Nadirah Nasir (9)
The Willow Primary School, Tottenham

Peculiar Pets

I am a big brown dog, with big
Fluffy hair, I have wings on the side
Like a horse named Pegasus.

I am cute, grumpy, and most importantly
A fabulous dog. *Ruff ruff!* I like to fly amongst
The clouds with my marvellous hump on my
incredible back.

My claws are like chainsaws
Cutting the tree so I could viper my enemy
I am a wild animal flying through
Tight spaces.

Matas Lisauskas (10)
The Willow Primary School, Tottenham

Goldy And Peks

My fish are Goldy and Peks.
Goldy is the oldest and Goldy is shy.
(Don't tell him that I said that)
Peks looks after his older brother Goldy.
Peks is the bravest,
They love me and I love them.

I had a cat called Nila.
She had eight babies.
I never got to see her much because she was as
fast as lightning.
I will never forget her.
And yay! We might get a rabbit next!

Krisharn Clarke (9)

The Willow Primary School, Tottenham

Pandycorn

P andycorn is its name

A cuddly, incredible creature she appears to be

N eon purple is her fluffy fur

D aring and kind is her character

Y et so pure don't be deceived

'C ause in the night she becomes a cunning villain

O h! Its cuteness is its weapon

R otten is its crumbling heart

N onetheless, I love my amazing Pandycorn!

Phoebe Oduro-Kwarteng (10)

The Willow Primary School, Tottenham

Fluffy The Bunny

Fluffy the bunny
O, Fluffy bunny
How you are my special friend
And how you blend,
Blend in with the clouds
Cute as you can be
However, when you open your dear mouth
Whoever sees you, will shout
As your teeth are as long as my arm
Seeing your smirk
As people run,
Knowing of their mistake,
Argh!
People scream from the terror of
Fluffy the bunny.

Stefania Turlea (11)
The Willow Primary School, Tottenham

My Incredible Dog

My dog is called Sunstar because when it is morning, his hair turns dazzling gold.
When the sun shines upon him, his hair dazzles in the sunlight.
Then when it is night, his hair turns midnight blue.
The moon and the stars in the evening add an extra special something...
They turn his hair brown with tiny little dazzling stars.
What a special dog I have!

Hadassa Kabuiku (9)
The Willow Primary School, Tottenham

Hyper Husky

H usky, I adore.
Y ellow bed,
P urple hat,
E nergetic mind,
R ed eyes.

H e's my hyper husky.
U nder my table, it's a hyper world.
S ometimes, I wonder what's going on in his head.
K eep hearing bark! Bark!
Y et, I still adore my hyper husky.

Luis Ciku (9)
The Willow Primary School, Tottenham

Dinersaur

D inersaur is very short,

I t's a very short dinosaur.

N ot a biting but a dancing dinosaur.

E ats on a dinner table.

R ages when he loses a game.

S mells really good.

A t a garden,

U nder a gnome.

R uins parties every time if you are with the dinersaur.

Zhir Mahdi-Outhman (9)

The Willow Primary School, Tottenham

Bug The Pug

B ug is my special pug.
U nderground he digs,
G oing in the tunnel and

T asting the impure air.
H owling at the sky,
E ager to play.

P iling up speed,
U rging to have fun,
G ifted with energy, my very special pug.

Jayden Taylor-Macauley (10)
The Willow Primary School, Tottenham

Crocky The Hero

C rocky is the best hero of all

R eady to fight crime any time!

O h, he sure is cute with them bright green eyes

C rocky loves everyone no matter what!

K arma is what he gives to the criminals

Y eah, he's a crocodile but he can save the day!

Kaan Mustafa (11)

The Willow Primary School, Tottenham

Mitten

M itten is a fluffy, cute cat.

I t likes to sleep during the day.

T onight she will wake

T hen have a party for cats.

E nding it will be hard because Mitten is aggressive.

N ever-ending parties are annoying!

Selnur Sari (9)
The Willow Primary School, Tottenham

The Catagroo

The Catagroo lives in the jungle deep
Away from civilisation for all it does is sleep
But when the sun is low at a very certain time
The Catagroo comes out for dinner
At the clock bell chime
Then it goes to bed
For midnight is up ahead.

Jamil Al-Abbas (10)
The Willow Primary School, Tottenham

Rockstar Marvin

A kennings poem

Guitar player
Tree climber
Raucous singer
Tail hanger
Funky dancer
Tree swinger
Head banger
Nit picker
Leather wearer
Banana lover
Sunglass sporter
Primate triber
Mischievous Rockstar Monkey Marvin.

Frankie Le May (10)
The Willow Primary School, Tottenham

Pitten

P itten is a rare pet

I t lives in a field

T ender food is what it enjoys

T alent is what it has

E ating a lot is its special talent

N o one has a pitten like mine, it's my secret pet.

Abigail Ochan (10)

The Willow Primary School, Tottenham

My Cat - Prince, The Superhero

What's my name?
I'm Super Prince the cat.

I can fly, I can dry!
But I can die and survive.
I'm Super Prince!
If you need me, call my name: Super Prince.
I will be there straight away!

Anthony Corcoran (10)
The Willow Primary School, Tottenham

Tauro

T rickster is as clever as a fully-developed human.

A nxious as a mouse.

U npredictable like an undiscovered animal.

R esilient as a worker ant.

O ptimistic as a leader.

Ranveer Singh (10)

The Willow Primary School, Tottenham

The Fire Flamingo

Its legs look like a wire on fire.
Its wings look like springs.
It can fly so high, it can nearly touch the sky.
Its feathers are red and soft like a bed.
Its beak is very unique.

Shanaiya Theodoulou (9)
The Willow Primary School, Tottenham

Crazy Little Cat!

Oh, look!
There's a cat.
Is it chasing a hat?
Maybe it's looking for a rat.
Oh! It wants a mat.
Crazy little cat!

Zeynep Gunes (11)
The Willow Primary School, Tottenham

Flame The Firecorn

F lame is famous for her fire,

L eaping over lakes and seas,

A iming for her giant lair,

M ice and rats shriek and scatter away as she enters,

E eks and shrieks come from the streets,

T iresome work being Flame,

H eat and lava in her veins,

E very day she gets pushed away,

F irecorns are very rare,

I t might take years to find one,

R ising from the lava lake,

E lephants are tiny in comparison to firecorns,

C akes and bakes are her favourite treat,

O nly water can stop this creature,

R unning water is her least favourite thing,

N ot one human can go near them, only other creatures can!

Effie Lunn (10)

The Winchcombe School, Shaw Estate

Awesome Arnie: Hero Hound

Awesome Arnie: hero hound, can leap tall buildings in a single bound.
With his super ears, he patrols the skies,
Swooping,
Soaring,
Until he spies...

Cunning Crow and his evil mob,
Ganging up on a defenceless mog.

"Hand over your food," said the nasty bird,
"because if you don't, I'm sure you've heard,
Of the mean and nasty things I do to people just like you."

"Leave me alone you mean old crow, I have no food as I'm sure you know.
You took it all yesterday."
"Then," said Crow, "you'll have to pay!"

Crow and crew advanced on him, but then they
heard a familiar din,
Our hero hound had swung a punch, directed at
Crow's evil bunch.

"Take that!" said Arnie. "Leave him alone, he is
with me, now go on home!"
"It's Awesome Arnie!" Crow's crew cried as they
scampered off to hide, Except for Crow who stood
his ground, defiant of our super hound.
"Push off," said Crow. "You're no match for us,"
then he turned around and saw the dust...
That his crew had left behind when they ran off to
hide.

Realising he was on his own, cunning Crow flew off
and moaned,
"Darn you, Arnie, foiled again. I'll win one day, and
that will be the end.
And on that day you will see, that you are no
better than me."

"Thank you, Arnie" replied the mog. "You really are
my super dog!"

"No need for thanks," our dog replied and up in the sky, he started to glide.
Arnie had a massive grin as his blue cape fluttered in the wind.

Oliver Oakham (9)

The Winchcombe School, Shaw Estate

Grumpy Herman

G rubby grumpy Herman has never looked divine

R ed has been his favourite colour since turning nine

U pstairs is where he eats his food

M y friends rarely touch him as he's always in a mood

P ets are always cute but my tortoise is not

Y ou might not agree but calling him grumpy is a lot

H ey it's not that I'm complaining as I love him a bunch

E very day I hear him go... munch... munch... munch...

R eally I call him Hermy Wormy as it's such a better name

M any times I say this but he has driven me insane

A lways remember pets are loved just the way they are

N ow I have to say that I love him every day and every hour.

Bethany Lloyd (10)
The Winchcombe School, Shaw Estate

Magical Maxie

Magical Maxie, my peculiar pet,
Most adorable rabbit I have ever met.
What's so special about her?
Is it her white fluffy fur?
That's not it, she can actually fly!
Fluttering around the bright blue sky!
No, she does not carry wings,
Neither a wand that sings.
Her magical suit is what she needs,
Soaring high in supersonic speeds.
That made her so proud,
That she grew rude and loud.
She's no longer nice, caring and kind.
The sweet Maxie I got home, I could not find!

When she woke up one morning,
I could hear her sobbing!
"What's the matter, Maxie, my dear?"
"My suit, I have lost," she said in fear.
"I can never fly around!
Have to just stay on the ground.

That's the end of my magic!
What could be more tragic?"
She was upset all day,
Still in her cage, locked away.
I went to her and said, "My honey,
The magic doesn't really bother me!
I still love you as before,
Whether you are in the skies or on the floor."

She realised the value of love,
And her magical suit over and above,
Promised to herself to be the sweetest ever,
"My magical suit I can forget, never."
Lo and behold, the magical suit was home!
We thought it'd vanished in foam.
She was filled with joy and pleasure,
To find her magical treasure.
She never took it off, but for at night!
Always clinging to it, so tight.
Happy to find my sweet Maxie near!
Magical she is, adorable and dear!
Magical Maxie, my peculiar pet,
Most adorable rabbit I have ever met.

Akshara Shivakumar (9)

The Winchcombe School, Shaw Estate

You've Got A Friend In Me

A bird flew to his nest to have a rest.
He always flew high in the sky.

His bird belly is shaped like a nut, so I called him
Peanut.
He's got fluffy, rainbow wings and a tiny, funny
head
And that all together makes him look perfect!

His nest is in a tree and he's always looking at me.
The tree is in my backyard and it's taller than me.
It's such a big tree!

One night, he came to my window and knocked to
wake me up.
He started talking like crazy because he thinks my
dog is lazy.
The house is not protected so Peanut cannot rest.
He's such a mess!

I tried to calm him down. I don't want him to
stress.
I took him to my bed, to let him have a rest.

In the morning, he woke up and was flying around like crazy.
He sang 'I Believe I Can Fly' and it looked amazing!

Finally, I had to stop him, before he got a dizzy head.
"I've never seen a talking bird. Do you want to be my peculiar pet?"

Silly little Peanut, you are a little crazy but
I really like you so it will be amazing!

We are now friends and he lives with me.
Every day we sing together 'You've Got a Friend In Me'.

Alex Skrodzki (9)
The Winchcombe School, Shaw Estate

Colin The Cat

Yes, I know, it's such a shame,
about our pet cat Colin's name.

He's not the most friendly of cats,
but to be honest we really don't mind that.
He was born in a barn and can be quite wild,
sometimes his scratches sting and sometimes they
are quite mild.

Colin sits all day in the chair,
and when you get near him he gives you a death
stare.

Our cat is sixteen years young and he used to be a
lot of fun.

Racing round the house, chasing his toy mouse.
Up and down the stairs, leaving lots of cat hair.

Now Colin is slowing down, he spends most of his
days sleeping,
and if he is awake, you will usually find him eating.
He's not keen on his own cat food,
but he does sit at the table with us when he is in
the mood.

He likes to eat cheese and ice cream,
I think it gives him funny dreams.

He is a very peculiar cat, but we love him and that
is that.

James Renaut (10)
The Winchcombe School, Shaw Estate

How Pebbles Changed The World

Have you ever wondered,
What your dog could do
If those old folk tales,
Were ever really true?

Well let me tell you personally,
About a special dog,
A dog whose name was Pebbles,
Who was the size of a frog.

She was sitting by the table,
On that very fateful day,
Wondering: *how can I get this food,*
Is there a proper way?

Suddenly, she had an idea,
One that changed the world,
What if she could use her cuteness,
Making the task look absurd?

Thinking of all her sadness,
She blinked up at the table,
Entrancing all of the humans,
Making their thoughts unstable.

Before she even knew it,
'Puppy eyes' was born,
Giving her the power
To keep her stomach filled and warm.

Emilia Muryn (10)
The Winchcombe School, Shaw Estate

The Giraffe Who Couldn't Stop Dancing

From the day it was born,
It was always dancing,
Even if her skirt was torn,
She kept on prancing.

Day and night,
People would watch with cheer,
To some people, it is the light,
Of a day filled with tears.

It has won the world record,
For being the only animal to be able to do a spin,
Everyone who watches looks at her in awe,
And every contest she goes to she always wins.

No one knows where the talent originated,
For her parents are perfectly normal giraffes,
But until we find the answer to where the talent is created,
We can carry on listening to the dance pieces it crafts.

Shreeya Agarwala (9)
The Winchcombe School, Shaw Estate

Harry The Hip-Hop Hippo

I have a pet named Harry and he's very peculiar.
You see he's a hippo (which is cool) but there's
something even cooler!

Harry is a hip-hop star when he's not being my pet.
He tours around the world in his own private jet.

He lives in my back garden and writes his own
raps.
But comes inside to eat his favourite ham and
cheese baps.

I always listen to his music when I'm feeling bored,
And I get to go to the shows where he wins his
awards.

I love him very much, he's really very funny.
He's lovable, he's talented and he's my best buddy.

Isaac Pearton (9)
The Winchcombe School, Shaw Estate

My Pet Wame

I never had a special friend,
Until the day he came,
Not like any normal pet,
My one and only Wame.

He has a funny, furry face,
Though the rest of him is bald,
He's great at making sandwiches,
And stops me getting cold.

He's big but not gigantic,
He's clever, cute and tame,
My pet is named Despacito,
My slowly crawling Wame.

He's loyal and he's caring,
A most peculiar pet,
Always by my side,
My best companion yet!

Alice Smith (10)
The Winchcombe School, Shaw Estate

My Pet Chamturt

My pet's name is Chamturt,
But his nickname is Burt,
He can camouflage any colour to hide,
And even have different colours each side.
He is cute, clever, colourful and tame,
No other creature is the same.
I'm trying to teach him how to speak
And our favourite game is hide-and-seek.
He sometimes hides under my winter hat
To get away from the neighbour's cat.
Last week he went invisible to escape the vet,
But overall he's the best peculiar pet.

Rudi Frampton (10)
The Winchcombe School, Shaw Estate

My Peculiar Pet Fluffball

F luffball is a small ball of fluff,

L ittle and warm to fit in my pocket,

U nleashed on the ground, he shuffles and bounces like a ball,

F luffing up to keep my hands warm,

F urry friend changes colour in the sunlight from white to yellow,

B ig wide eyes looking at you so cute,

A lways ready for a hug,

L ikes to feed on candyfloss,

L oving little creature to hang out with.

Chester Dry (10)

The Winchcombe School, Shaw Estate

Bob The Brave Hamster

I have a brave little hamster, Bob,
Who sizzles non-stop,
His nose is constantly moving
As if he were just sniffing all day long.
His tail is small, barely visible,
And if he just has no better thing to do,
He plays with his friend Popp.
But he's not just any hamster!
He becomes invisible at night,
And rallies in the apartment with his turbo-
powered
Hot Wheels car and then races down the street all
night long.

Alehandro Abdelhamed (10)

The Winchcombe School, Shaw Estate

Sparkle The Unicorn Queen

Sparkle is a sparkly, rainbow unicorn queen.
Sparkle is the queen of Imagine Land.
She has a little girl called Jem.
She loves flying through the night sky and doing loop the loops.
Guards surround the rainbow palace.
All her unicorns respect her and Sparkle respects them back.
Sparkle helps her fellow unicorns if any of them need help.

Amelia Newbery (10)
The Winchcombe School, Shaw Estate

My Peculiar Pet

I own a peculiar pet,
Can you guess what it is?

It has a back like a boulder and sharp long claws.
Beaming black eyes and snappy jaws.
Its legs are quite lumpy,
And it's often quite grumpy.
My, oh my, what could it be?
Are you a little bit nervous to see?

Oh, phew!
It's only a tortoise.

Toby Thorp (10)
The Winchcombe School, Shaw Estate

What Tiger

Tiger, tiger, out at night
Tiger, tiger, burning bright
This tiger wants a cuddle
But doesn't want to walk in a puddle
Whiskers only wants a friend
But all people want to do is chuck him in a bend
Then he got care
And found out his owner was a billionaire.

Amelia Brunsden (10)
The Winchcombe School, Shaw Estate

Purrfect Song

This is the most hilarious song my cat has ever
written.
Even though it is a three-month-old kitten.
I am Elly's intelligent and favourite cat.
And I play instruments wherever I'm sat.
I will not sit on a rusty, old mat!
As it is very, very flat!

Elly Wong (10)
The Winchcombe School, Shaw Estate

My Pug

My pug's name is Charlie.
My dog is a fatty
Because my brother gives him a lot of patties.
He loves peanut butter from the Kong.
He is as big as Donkey Kong.
He likes to lick.
He sticks to my mum
Because, well, he gets cuddles!

Jack Smith (10)
The Winchcombe School, Shaw Estate

My Slimy Snail

My name's Speedy,
Please can you feed me,
I don't need a lead,
As I'm not often freed,
I think I'm fine,
But I make lots of slime,
I came in the mail,
When I was a baby snail.

Lorri Harper (10)
The Winchcombe School, Shaw Estate

My Pet Snake Harry

H arry is a harmless python

A baby one, if you will

R eally he is just a snake, he is harmless

R eady, Harry? Let's go

Y es, I take my snake on walks.

Connor Jones (9)

The Winchcombe School, Shaw Estate

The Dog Cat

There is a Dog Cat called Frank
He is as long as a plank
He is the colour of the sun
And he loves to have fun
Except when he's done
He lies in his bed like a sausage in a bun.

Charlie Bortoli-Holmes (10)
The Winchcombe School, Shaw Estate

My Pet Snoopy

Snoopy is an amazing koala
He is a very brilliant drummer!
He loves to drum and also listens to a lot of rock music
He loves to play and make new friends
And he especially loves to write with me
He loves making mystery stories!
Snoopy loves to use his imagination.

S pecial
N eighbourly
O utstanding
O pen-minded
P lacid
Y oung.

Elizabeth Ikuesan (9)
Uphall Primary School, Ilford

Chick The Spy

He runs on his little feet,
Toppling over whoever he meets,
He has the agility of a nimble cheetah,
Some people say he might be a ninja!

Despite his size, he always wins
Even if the opponent is as big as five bins!
He's as black as the moon, so you never see him coming
Bash! And you're already running!

He uses his wings to slice and dice,
He's so strong he can cut through ice!
His bloodshot eyes leave you stuck,
If you want to escape you need pure luck!

Chick the spy is the absolute best,
He'll run all the way to Budapest.
Chick the spy, he never fails,

Scratch! And he's beaten you with nails.

Muhammad Zubair (11)
Valence Primary School, Dagenham

Adventures Of Ella The School Dog

Ella comes bounding down the corridor at 7:30 am,
Leash off and a good shake of her fur,
Spraying puffs of snow up in the air.

Ms Bailey gives the command: "Go see Janet!"
And off Ella bolts, like lightning from another planet.
She leaps up onto Janet's lap
Who is busy at the computer, going tap, tap, tap.

Wriggling and squirming, Ella fits herself in
Reaches up and gives Janet a lick on the chin.
Janet smiles and so the day begins,
Ella's ability to spread joy is always a win.

Next stop is Shannon, who is in Year 2,
Ella enjoys her lessons
All of which is true.
It is but a pit stop for a quick Shannon-cuddle
And off Ella goes as the children get in a huddle.

Her all-time favourite is of course Aunty Julie in
Reception
Where Ella becomes Choochie Mama according to
Julie's perception.
She fills her up with treats and cuddles galore
Ella looks up at Julie as the one she adores.

What about the children, you say?
We will get to that later in the day.
Off Ella trots to Tracy Shelley
Who comes across as aloof
But Ella knows that she is Tracy's favourite floof.

Controlled by the needs of her belly,
Ella contemplates her next stop.
Oh yes, how could we forget, Y6 to Sue Chafer
She's definitely got some treats, maybe a doggy
wafer.
With her puppy dog eyes, Ella dazzles
Raises a paw and Sue is bedazzled.

Where to next?
Oh yes, the office of Beth.
Ella's 'go to' place to get her pampering needs
met.

Unless of course, she bumps into Vicky Goode, the office lady
Who insists on carrying Ella like a baby
Rocking her from side to side
Accompanied by a smile so wide.

Ella Bailey (7)
Valence Primary School, Dagenham

Merlin

We've all been to a zoo before.
Seen all the animals roam.
From slippery snakes and cheeky monkeys
To penguins in their icy dome.

Yet I don't need to go to a zoo,
To hear a lion roar.
As it can be heard if you go upstairs,
And check inside my sock drawer!

My little kitty is very peculiar.
She is not your everyday cat.
She changes colours, depending on her mood,
And sleeps in my dad's red woolly hat.

Now, I know you may be wondering,
How on earth does she change colour?
I'm afraid I don't know how to answer that,
But I can tell you that I love her.

Amira Ali (11)
Valence Primary School, Dagenham

Bloop Bop Blop Bim

I have met a peculiar pet,
He's short, he's yellow, he said to me hello!
The owner said that I could have him, she said that
he was a bloop bop blop bim
I bought him food, I bought a lot
I thought he'd like it but he did not
Then he said he wanted to eat me!
So I ran and I ran, all the way home...
But I didn't have my key
I pounded on the door, I pounded hard
I could see my pet running through the yard,
But then the earth started swirling around and
around,
I woke up from my dream, and my dog came on to
my bed with a bound.

Ria Day (10)
Valence Primary School, Dagenham

The Running Racoon

T he running racoon you have never ever seen.
H e has never stopped running.
E ven at night.

R unning today.
U nfortunately sometimes when the gym closes he has to run on a treadmill.
N ever on grass also
N ever on trees.
I mposing as a sports car.
N ot like a bug.
G reat like Albert Einstein.

R uns at a marathon,
A t a gym,
C orridor,
O lympics,
O ver the mountains,
N ever in the sea.

Faaiz (7)

Valence Primary School, Dagenham

Wonderland Forest

In the wonderland forest, the green grass grows
Beauty around you wherever you go
But inside the tree, not a squirrel or owl
Instead, you will see a calabocow
And not a bird or fly
But a colourful monkey flying high in the sky
Between the grass, not a snake or bug
But if you follow the slime you will find a bright
blue slug
And in the middle of nowhere, not a house or a hut
But a tree that is covered in fluff
The wonderland is where your imagination grows
And if you like beauty then it's where to go.

Nina Booysen (10)
Valence Primary School, Dagenham

The Rainbow Rainbird

R ainbird is very rare, when it touches you, you can make a wish.

A rainbird can make a rainbow that fades as it flies.

I think it's real. But is it? If it is, it's my pet.

N ever catch a rainbird as it flies by.

B ecause it needs to come to you.

I f you believe it's real, then it is.

R ainbird can make a rainbow inside your house and it will stay there for two weeks.

D id you know that if you make a rainbird wish you can understand all rainbirds?

Maxim Hristov (7)

Valence Primary School, Dagenham

G Is For Guinea Pigs

G uinea pigs are cute and don't like to get wet
U p at dawn and ready to play
I 'd love one as a pet
N ice and friendly they are
E ating fruits and vegetables, what a little star
A nd if you let them outside, I'm sure they won't go far

P erfect pets they can be
I n pairs they like to live, so they don't get lonely
G ood to have as your very first pet
S o you can have a furry friend you won't forget.

Leah Palmer (11)
Valence Primary School, Dagenham

Grace The Gymnast

Grace is a dog that's nine years old
She is a gymnast
You're probably thinking how is a dog a gymnast?
Well, she is extraordinary
That's right, extraordinary
She can do a handstand, walk on her hands, say
no more!

One day, Grace went to doggie boggie (dog gym)
She did tricks and flips
Until she fell down
She got rushed to the vet
They found out one of Grace's paw got lost
Ever since she has been
The one-hand doggy!

Laura Ameny (9)
Valence Primary School, Dagenham

My Pet Rainboom

R ainboom is so fast, she can do a sonic rainboom.

A rainboom means that a pony flies so fast that makes a big blast of rainbow everywhere.

I love my pet Rainboom.

N ight-time, she comes out and makes the moon glow.

B elieve she can make the sun rainbow.

O n the first day of summer, she makes the world warm.

O nly this pony can make a rainbow.

M agic rainboom pets only come to you if you can see a rainboom.

Isabella Hristova (7)

Valence Primary School, Dagenham

My Chinchilla

My chinchilla,
His name is Chinchilly
He has a big diet of rice
And he smears it on a lion!

My chinchilla
Has black and white fur
Like a zebra riding around the world
Shining from afar!

My chinchilla,
He looks at me with love
Like I'm his mother
Caring for him.

My chinchilla,
His name is Chinchilly
He acts a bit silly
My chinchilla is the best in the world...

Azzam Gardaizi (11)
Valence Primary School, Dagenham

Jumbojeti

J et speed is how fast he is.

U nbelievable amount of collars,

M unching on his food as quiet as a mouse.

B umblebees drop to the ground as soon as they see him.

O h and how amazing he is!

J aguars run away as soon as he is in sight.

E ating at least a kilogram of food a day;

T he Great Fire of London won't even hurt him,

I love him so much!

Andrei Cheaburu Maiu (7)

Valence Primary School, Dagenham

Majestic Cambird!

My Cambird is golden like the sand
Camel and bird go hand in hand

When it runs it sounds like a band
Its wings spread out, across the land

Its leathery wings push it high in the air
Before coming back down into its lair

It eats creepy crawlies off the desert floor
It cracks them open using its claws

This is my peculiar pet
Who never needs to go to the vet.

Haris Abbas (10)
Valence Primary School, Dagenham

Pokémon

My pet rat is...

Yellow and black
Its yellow and black face has red spots
And its yellow and black tail is a lighting bolt
It fires lighting from its tail
My yellow and black pet has small paws
We look in awe as my pet plays all over our yellow house
Breaking everything in its path.
Ow, I fell, what is this?
Oh no, it's a nuke!
Boom!

Thomas Bampoe (11)
Valence Primary School, Dagenham

My Pet Serpent

My pet serpent is not anything like a devil's serpent.
It's a sweet thing, it deserves to be a king
Everybody thinks he is scary, but no, it's as sweet as a cherry
It can help you in lots of things, it can even help you find your lost rings!
It can make you popcorn because that's how helpful it was born
He is very nice, so he deserves some ice.

Edona Krasniqi (10)
Valence Primary School, Dagenham

Fantastic Fang

My Fang is so cool,
One day he will rule,
All over the world, in his car,
He might go long, he might go far,

My hamster Fang is so awesome,
If he were a dinosaur, he would be roar-some,
He is strong and never wrong,

Fang, my friend, you are sweet,
You are a true friend and can not be beat.

Alfie Reid-Miles (10)
Valence Primary School, Dagenham

My Cat Ramses

I was upstairs, reading my book on the stairs,
And my mum called me... "Look!"
There was a kitten, with a jumper knitted,
He was so fluffy and lonely.
We named him Ramses,
And this little kitten with a jumper knitted is now
playing with me...
Yes, all day playing and chasing.

Anastasija Gurska (9)
Valence Primary School, Dagenham

World Record Otter

My pet would be a world record otter!
It would be good at anything and do human stuff!
It would keep on breaking world records
On many things like swimming, climbing and more!
It would be the most famous otter!

Matas Tamasauskas (11)
Valence Primary School, Dagenham

About Fluffy

F antastic elephant teddy.

L ovely and nice she is.

U nique and helpful.

F un to play with.

F unny too.

Y ou'd love to be her owner, wouldn't you?

Emily Nicholas (8)

Valence Primary School, Dagenham

Sloth

S haggy fur
L ive in the tropical forests of central South America
O ften sit hanging upside down
T hey can be 2 to 2.5 feet
H eads sad-looking eyes and tiny ears.

Maria Lee (7)
Valence Primary School, Dagenham

My Dogecorn

D oes eat plants
O h, everyone loves him
G ood boy!
E asy to train
C ould he jump high?
O f course he can!
R ural
N ever naughty.

Freddie Jones (11)
Valence Primary School, Dagenham

Puppies Are The Best

P uppies are cute
U sually they are snuggly
P retty and sweet
P ugs are very sneaky
Y ou better get a puppy because they keep you company.

Megan Palmer (7)
Valence Primary School, Dagenham

My Imaginary Pet

Bambis are scared when someone is looking at them
Elephants are very strong
Leopards hunt for prey
Lions are the kings of the forest
Anteaters look for ants to eat.

Claire Angulo-Quesada (7)

Valence Primary School, Dagenham

Perfect Peek A Boo

She's awesome and kind
And loves fighting crime
She's got a big heart
That's what sets her apart
From all her friends
And the ones that pretend
She turns in a flash
To let out her fashion
She flies up above
Like a dove with love

One second she's there
The next she isn't
But always makes sure
That she's present
In her natural form or no form at all
She's peek a *boo*, peek a *boo*, peek peek peek a
Boo!

She loves eating stew
And never catches the flu
She has not one clue

That she just flew right above you
Did you see her crew?
No 'cause she has not one cool dude
Since all of them are rude
Last time she was viewed

She had a peculiar attitude
Don't worry, now she's changed her mood
And has never got sued
Now let's see how she has improved

P erfect
E xcellent
E nergetic
K ind

A wesome

B eautiful
O bedient
O bliging.

You see, it all really is just in her name
No wonder why she has so much fame
She really does have the perfect aim

In every concert that she plays
She keeps her bunny ears high
Has not the slightest touch of shy
Never shows off any of her pride

Just one look in her eye
And you'll start to cry
Maybe it is time to say bye-bye
Oh I just love how she is so cute
Okaaaay okaaaayyyy...
We'll go back on mute!

Jarrah Wajiha (10)
Vicarage Primary School, East Ham

The Panird!

The bird can fly like it's never been happier,
The bird can cry like it's never been sadder,
The bird can do anything on its own,
Like it's never had money to owe!

The panda can eat like *chomp! Chomp! Chomp!*
The panda can complete anything like *chop! Chop! Chop!*
The panda can do anything on its own,
Like it's never had money to owe!

The bird can talk like *chirp! Chirp! Chirp!*
The bird can walk like *stomp! Stomp! Stomp!*
The bird can do anything on its own,
Like it's never had money to owe!

The bird can do anything like a panda,
The panda can do anything like a bird,
Both animals can do anything on their own,
Like they've never had money to owe!

It's the panird!

Maliha Chowdhury (10)
Vicarage Primary School, East Ham

Last Night, I Saw My House Alive

The doors were dancing like a dazzling damsel
As the chandeliers were singing like a peacock in Brazil
The curtains were running like a cheetah after prey
While the table was waiting for a beautiful display

The vase was sleeping like a peaceful cat
While the bed was breathing as it lay on a designer mat
The fan was confused as it went round and round and round
While the washing machine was screaming until all the clothes were found

The walls marched and stampeded around the house
While the lamp looked down and moved around

The garden talked to all the trees
Making itself known to all that sees
While all the butterflies played with the bees.

Hadiya Fahad (9)
Vicarage Primary School, East Ham

Last Night, I Saw The Classroom Alive

Last night, I saw the classroom alive
Doors opening and closing
Laughing loudly and proudly

Last night, I saw the classroom dancing
Rulers crashing and bashing
Rubbers dancing and advancing through the night

Last night, I saw the classroom shining
Glitter sprinkled across the horizon
Taking me away, far away

Last night, I saw the classroom fighting
Pens and pencils bickering
Jumping in and out of pots while bumping.

Ziya Ishaq (10)
Vicarage Primary School, East Ham

My Weird But Rather Useful Pet

Fifteen eyes for looking around
Everything all found
From teddies to books
If you look at it may be creepy
But definitely cool

Seventeen legs for running
For tag and from police
Stealing an art piece
Would now be a breeze

Nineteen personalities
Ninety identities
The most confusing pet in the world
It may be anyone
So look at your friend
And look at this peculiar pet

May have at least two of everything
Making himself useful
But don't forget
It still has one heart only.

Jason John Selvakumar (10)
Vicarage Primary School, East Ham

The Mysterious Cat Hero

There the cat goes
Her cape blows
Her shoes glow
She will take her leave and go
Villains say bye
Then she will fly

Into the night
She will fight
For what's right
She is a cat knight
Then she will take flight

They won't stop her
She wears her disguise forever
She will never surrender
Protecting her owner
Villains, she will always remember

This was a story of a cat hero
Never zero
Always there
Never scared.

Kaydie Laing (11)
Vicarage Primary School, East Ham

Dribbles

D ribbles is an odd, clumsy, excitable and extraordinary genie.

R eal genies like Dribbles are as messy as children with paint.

I am his owner, my name is William.

B illy came to see Dribbles and William, Billy wanted to make a wonderful wish.

B illy asked Dribbles for a new car but instead Dribbles splatted Billy on the face with toothpaste.

L illy came to make a wish with Dribbles, she wished for a husband and she got splatted too.

E veryone who asked Dribbles for anything got splatted.

S top, stop, stop, no more wishes from Dribbles, it is too messy, no more!

William Wedd-Johnson (8)

Watlington Community Primary School, Watlington

Savanah The Zebracorn

Z ebracorns are sweet and special.

E specially colourful and cuddly.

B ut they can be naughty and the

R est of the time they are good. Savanah is my favourite Zebracorn.

A lso, Savanah can be mischievous when playing with the other Zebracorns.

C ute and caring Savanah is when I play with her.

O scar is Savanah's brother; her mum and dad are called

R ex and

N atalie, they love playing together day and night, if you stay up, you might just see them.

Eloise Farr (9)

Watlington Community Primary School, Watlington

Reggae Rick The Sloth

R eggae is the type of music Rick writes and performs.

E very day Rick practises his singing.

G rapes are his favourite food.

G as machines are often used in his performances.

A favourite song of his is 'Buffalo Soldier' by Bob Marley.

E veryone loves him.

R ick loves Bob Marley.

I nvitations are sent out for his concerts.

C razy and wild is his style.

K is the last letter of his name.

Marley Bellamy (9)

Watlington Community Primary School, Watlington

The Woof Quacky

W oof Quacky the ninja dog duck!

O h no! Woof Quacky strikes again. *Woof, quack, woof!*

O ften Woof Quacky is saving the day, but today he is hungry.

"F ood," says Woof Quacky!

Q uick, run after the food!

U p, up and away flies Woof Quacky.

"A ttack, get the bread, I need food!" shouts Woof Quacky!

C ome to me, food!

K eep the bread, Woof Quacky.

Y ay, yum, yum, yum.

Imogen Roythorne (8)

Watlington Community Primary School, Watlington

Bob The Tortoise

Bob the unusual tortoise was wearing a colourful
jacket
That came from a very small packet.
Bob was very merry when slowly wandering
through the woods with his tiny hood up.
Bob had a very unusual pattern
On his jacket that reminded him of the planet
Saturn.
Bob came to a shed,
Where he settled for bed.
Bob then dreamed of
Corn on the cob.
Then all of a sudden he fell out of bed
And banged his head on the shed.

Jack Hansell (9)
Watlington Community Primary School, Watlington

DJ's Story

My pet DJ Sloth was very, very sneezy when he was about to rock out.
His friend, Sid the cat, sat on his hat and everything went downhill from there.
The microphone tipped and landed on Sid and Bagel the Beagle sat on an eagle.
The eagle flipped out and started to pout.
The stage fell down all crumpled up and that was the end of that.

Ellie Folland (8)
Watlington Community Primary School, Watlington

Max Is A Hero

M arvellous Max is brave

A nd fierce. He loves treats and food.

X mas time he would run and jump around.

I cky

S limy

A nd he was sticky all over

H ero Max

E xtraordinary

R olls around everywhere

O rdinary dog really.

Alexi Jane Mills (9)

Watlington Community Primary School, Watlington

Ziggy The Cat/Hamster

Z iggy is a lovely cat/hamster, she doesn't scratch or bite

I n the igloo bed was Ziggy

G iggling. Ziggy is a giggling cat/hamster.

G oldfish. Ziggy ate a goldfish.

Y o-yo. Ziggy likes to play with yo-yos.

Scarlett Cuthbert (8)

Watlington Community Primary School, Watlington

Fluffy Egg

F riendly and

L ovely

U nique in every way

F un and

F luffy

Y ours to fuss and play.

E veryone's favourite

G enerous with her love

G olden-hearted.

Lara Easter (8)

Watlington Community Primary School, Watlington

The Alien Cat

I can walk, I can talk
I'm an alien cat.
We live in houses, we live in caves,
That's our habitat.
I have four eyes, two ears, two antennae,
That's how I hear a rat.
I've got a sharp tail so that I can catch food
because...
I'm an alien cat!

Toby Cooper (9)

Werrington Community Primary School, Yeolmbridge

My Red Panda Pet

My pet is so strange,
It puts me in a daze.
Therapy I should arrange,
For my pet has made my head like a haze.

My pet can move objects with its mind,
To places where I cannot find.
He flies around the house,
Finding every mouse.

At night, he keeps me awake,
Very very late!
Every day I ask him, can he stop?
He says no as my reaction is funny to watch!

This morning he went missing,
It turns out, he was only fishing.
My crazy, psychic red panda pet,
Then refused to go to the vet.

He is as soft as a pillow,
I found him in an orchard of willow.

George Towler (11)
West Malling CE Primary School, West Malling

Ellie The Elephant Travels To England!

Ellie the elephant can travel the Earth,
It's a surprising skill she's had since birth.
When she sprays water from her trunk,
She teleports somewhere and lands with a thump!

One day she decided to travel to England,
For she wasn't interested in sun, sea and sand,
Nor did she want to freeze in Iceland,
Really, she wanted to see cities and farmland.

The water flew up
Then she landed with a bump!
Suddenly I turned to see,
My favourite baby elephant sitting next to me!

Ellie wanted to see the sights,
But first, she needed to stay a few nights.
She said it took two exhausting flights,
The last one especially took all her might.

Finally, we could teleport to London,
I was excited to have some fun.
First, we went on the London Eye,
Ellie was shaking, it was so high!

Next, she wanted to see Big Ben,
You'll never guess what happened then...
We teleported together once again
And landed in the middle of some important men.

Ellie the elephant can travel the Earth,
It's a surprising skill she's had since birth.
The delightful days she'd spent
Finally came and went.

As I left, I heard a sigh,
Ellie, my beautiful baby elephant said...
Goodbye.

Elsie Shaw (10)
West Malling CE Primary School, West Malling

Dolly Dream

Dolly Dream is my peculiar pet,
She is part fish but she's not been caught yet.

She can walk on land and deep in water,
Striped like a zebra and blows up like a puffer.

Her scales shimmer and shine like sparkling diamonds,
When she uses her powers, she glows and glistens.

With a silky, iridescent and flowing tail,
It blows in the wind like a delicate sail.

White webbed feet, bumpy and slimy,
Waddles like a penguin, grand and almighty.

Choose it wisely, nature or galaxies,
You may never leave, they are the boundaries.

You can take one friend inside the bubble,
If you break the rules there will be trouble.

The grass isn't always greener they say,
Your life will travel in a mysterious way,
Leave your old life behind today,
What will you choose, leave or stay?

Millie Stevens (11)
West Malling CE Primary School, West Malling

Darkness Turtle

Hi, I'm Nella the Darkness Turtle
And I passed my fear of the dark.
I go round and round, town to town,
Finding kids who need my shine.

I enter through the window,
The silence growing louder and louder,
I shine my neon shell
To shoo the nasty darkness hell.

There is truly nothing to worry about,
The darkness might give you a fright
But there is no need to worry
When you turn on the bright light.

You search the room,
Under the bed,
In the wardrobe,
In the cabinet,
Searching everywhere.

There is nothing here or there,
You can close your sleepy eyes
And rest your tired head,
If you're scared of the dark,
Just wait and see,
It might be you who will be seeing me!

Taliyah Seager
West Malling CE Primary School, West Malling

Sandy The Saviour

Sandy the Saviour is a top-notch dog,
Fearless and fast and very brave.
She bounces around just like a frog
But to be kind and helpful is her fave.

Her favourite thing is to go on walks,
When she sees someone sad,
She makes them feel glad.

She goes off to hospital glad and happy,
Making people very, very happy.
She licks them and hugs them
And loves healing their souls,
Making them able to reach their goals.

She will tuck you into bed
And turn off the lights,
Be there to protect you
From those scary nights.

She never rests until people are safe
As she knows we all have faith.
Sandy the Saviour - hero number one,
Never zero!

Jessica Diamond (11)
West Malling CE Primary School, West Malling

Cyril The Squirrel

I'm round and red and I laze in bed,
The treetop is where I call home,
Peering down at the humans on their phones.
Hiding nuts is what I do best
While the birds build their nests.

Spinning in circles, whirly-twirly to the ground,
Going in gardens, looking around.
Dogs come barking - oh, what a shock
As I turn them into big hard rock!

This is one of my secret powers
While I am picking my flowers.
I am cute and clever
Like a hairy feather.

I use my powers to sprint to a tree,
Oh, what a tale this has turned out to be!

Vinnie Goodayle (10)
West Malling CE Primary School, West Malling

Kind Koala

I am a koala - a kind koala,
I am soft like an ewok,
Strong like a hawk,
Cute like a puppy,
Smart like a human,
Look like a superhero,
My name is Kind Koala.

One touch of my tummy,
Brings joy and excitement
For you and all, forevermore.

You will shine like a star
And be asking for more,
But one touch is enough
For you and all.

I am Kind Koala, cute as can be,
To help you with your terrible deeds.
Now off I go to support more people,
Then, I am definitely going home!

Gideon Thornton (10)
West Malling CE Primary School, West Malling

Kung Fu Kangaroo!

Kung Fu Kangaroo!

Kung Fu Kangaroo,
Her dream is to row a boat.
Kung Fu Kangaroo,
But I think she's too heavy to float.

Kung Fu Kangaroo!

Kung Fu Kangaroo,
Really likes to box.
Kung Fu Kangaroo,
Wears multicoloured socks.
Kung Fu Kangaroo,
Has an enemy that's an ox.

Kung Fu Kangaroo!

Kung Fu Kangaroo,
Lives on Kanga Avenue.
Kung Fu Kangaroo,
Likes to chew on human shoes.

Kung Fu Kangaroo!

Kung Fu Kangaroo,
Has a joey named Roo.
Kung Fu Kangaroo,
Has a best friend that's a cockatoo.

Kung Fu Kangaroo!

Ava Barden (10)
West Malling CE Primary School, West Malling

Handy The Hawk

Handy the Hawk, he can teleport, and even help keep dimes.
With his wings he can fly and do a front flip to help save time.
He can run as fast as a bullet flying past, and even make Corona masks.

Handy the Hawk is always helpful,
Handy the Hawk is always careful,
Handy the Hawk with his super-sonic wings,
Electric dials to make his enemies fling.
Never fear, Handy the Hawk is here to make all your troubles go in a ping.

Kian Thorn (10)
West Malling CE Primary School, West Malling

Genie Giraffe

My pet is a genie giraffe,
He never wears a scarf,
He was born in Heaven,
But now lives in Devon,
He once ate my star graph.

Joseph Trott (11)
West Malling CE Primary School, West Malling

Sarah My Superhero Seahorse

My seahorse Sarah is a superhero
And she has a magic power source that is shaped like a zero,
Every night I help Sarah to the ocean
And when she dives in I can see her doing a special motion.
She has super hearing to hear the screams
Of the fish stuck in the rushing streams,
She is super fast and can get across the ocean in a dash
I think she is faster than the hero Flash
And when it's sunrise I come to Sarah very quick
And we run home as fast as a click.
The next day it ran by very fast
So at sunset, we went to the harbour in a dash,
But to our surprise, we came to see
Police tape covering the whole sea.
Sarah found a tiny gap
Yet she made it down in a snap.
She found a sign that warned her and she saw the biggest, baddest creature of all - the Kraken. She hid behind a rock

Then suddenly the rock became a door and it had
a special type of lock.
One minute later she found the key and she
opened the door
And she couldn't say anything anymore
It was a secret hideout, then she heard a blast
from the sidekicks in the past. They wanted to join
Sarah's gang
Then defeated the Kraken and the hero group was
called the Fang.
When I came from home at the docks
She brought the Fang and I was in shock.
I got over it very quick
And we went home in a flick.
And don't worry about the police tape
They removed it at a particular pace.

Zunaira Osman (8)
Wilbraham Primary School, Fallowfield

The Bluebird And The Beat

One day in the woodlands
A bluebird was chilling in its nest
It decided to have a fun fly around the woodlands
He met a wise bear, he wanted the bird to find him something
The bear said, "Blue little birdy, please get me something."
"Okay, what do you want? Honey?"
"Okay." Then he asked the bees,
"Hey guys, please
Can I have some honey?"
"Okay, sure."
The bird took the honey to the bear
"There you go."
"Hey, Beardo,
You want to come to my secret place?"
"Sure."
Then there it was, a secret beach

That same day,
They became
Friends forever.

Mali Aziz-Bernard (10)
Wilbraham Primary School, Fallowfield

My Purrr-Fect Mer-Cat

Meet my peculiar pet
Her name is Coral
The only cat who likes water
Because I'm the one who brought her
Back to the ocean with her family
Now they owe a lot to me.
She's the ruler, she's the monarch of underwater
She's part of the royal family now
She's got a whole new legacy
Because this is her long lost destiny.
And now I've gained a whole lot of popularity,
Now she is more independent
Because she's a descendant.
She now has lots of responsibility
She has bodyguards with a lot of hostility.
She's intelligent and equivalent, she's got agility
As this is democracy!

Zuhayra Osman (10)
Wilbraham Primary School, Fallowfield

My Pet Rabbit

I have a pet rabbit,
his name is Whiskers.
Every day he takes a sniff of my jacket.
He is a good listener.
He plays with gadgets,
and has earned a lot of badges.
He explores and travels around the planet.
He visited Italy,
and fed the pigeons individually.
Acting like a rockstar is his habit.
The best pet to have is Whiskers the rabbit!
His fur is soft and plushy,
when I talk to him, he gives me his concentration
fully.
He nibbles on my hair,
and shows me a lot of his care.
Disappointing me would be something he wouldn't
dare.
For him to bite, is really rare.
He plays in a band called the Bunny Beatles.
His favourite bird is an eagle.

Talia Kanadil (9)
Wilbraham Primary School, Fallowfield

My Polka Dot Girl

I have a little polka dot girl who dances when I twirl.
I would give away the world to have my little polka dot girl.
Her name is Snow Berry, a pretty strange name, huh,
But I like just the way it is for my polka dot girl.
People say I might be crazy, well...
It's better than owning a daisy
I like my polka dot girl just the way it is
And don't think you're ugly because I've experienced the same thing
Be animal kind
And just one day your animals will think that you're divine
I have a little polka dot girl that is
....
Human kind.

Nancy Mohammed (9)
Wilbraham Primary School, Fallowfield

Greg The Greedy Gorilla

Greg is a gorilla, a very greedy one indeed.
Yes, he is so greedy he eats apple seeds!
Greg has a superpower... in three seconds he can eat a hot dog,
Oh Greg, what a big hog!
Greg does not share
It's his worst nightmare.
This is a fact...
He can't even fit in the country's biggest potato sack!
He is so big
His head can't even fit in a gorilla-sized wig.
His belly is full of food
From all the steak he has chewed.
If you ever met Greg, what would you do?

Aaliyah Kennedy (9)
Wilbraham Primary School, Fallowfield

Kitty Cats

All cats are lazy but they like playing with you a lot
They play with your plants!
They like eating fish and raw bacon cat food
But most they like exploring the house
And seeing what their owners are doing,
When it's time to eat, cats smell the food and start
sniffing where it is coming from.
Thirty seconds after you put the food for the cats
they immediately come to eat.
Some cats in the world just like sleeping a lot but,
Most of them like staying and playing with their
owners.

Minna Abdelwahab (9)
Wilbraham Primary School, Fallowfield

The Lost Cat And The Nice Boy!

She, around her neck, has a big yellow bell,
When we went to the hotel,
I got her lost!
I can't tell you how much she cost!

I went around looking for her, crying and crying,
I was trying and trying...
To be brave.
What happiness she gave!

I asked and asked but came no reply,
So I guessed I would have to say goodbye.

I sat on a bench
And then came a boy who said he was French.
His name was Mat.
He had something in his hand... my cat!

Aqsa (11)
Wilbraham Primary School, Fallowfield

Elepheno

This is an animal, an elegant one
It's a great grey hunk
With a curly trunk
It's got great thick baggy knees
And it definitely has 0% fleas
Did you guess? Don't stress
It's an elephant, a big grey one
With a grey body and mighty tusks
Its fabulous strength is intense
And it drinks the water from the pond and
corresponds to everyone
But this elephant is not a normal one.

Nur Sabier (11)
Wilbraham Primary School, Fallowfield

We Are All Animal Kind!

My animal is rose gold.
My animal is far from cold.
My animal is my type.
She also thinks it's cool to write.
So does the company hype.
My animal has cyan spots.
Just like a dog's black, ordinary dots.
My animal is
Wise
Intelligent
Legendary
Luminous
Obliging
Whacky
And last of all, she is unique.
We are all unique.

Nadeem Mohammed (8)
Wilbraham Primary School, Fallowfield

The Saddest Polar Bear In The World!

The saddest polar bear in the world,
Sat there poorly uncurled.
He wondered about his weak childhood,
Thinking about it not being very good.
He went into his little snow-made house,
Inside he found a giant mouse.
He rested on his couch,
Other polars said he was a grouch.
There sat the saddest polar bear in the world,
Once again, uncurled.

Faryal Nawaz Khan Naz (11)
Wilbraham Primary School, Fallowfield

Jamie

J amie is kind-hearted, caring and doesn't lie

A nd has a heart of element and is as strong as gold, he

M ay be a long snake but who cares, we're all made

I n the end, he will be your life-long friend

E ither way, he will express himself to you so don't hurt his feelings, he has some too.

Lujaynah Abubaker (10)
Wilbraham Primary School, Fallowfield

Cat With A Wig

Of all the cats
Furball may not be the smartest of all the cats in
the world with wigs
I would count Furball to be the noisiest
But when I call her name
All she calls out is a quiet purr
And when I dream
I realise that maybe having a cat with a wig isn't
the most annoying.

Agnieszka Jonik (10)
Wilbraham Primary School, Fallowfield

My Pet Dog

My pet dog is big and fluffy
She loves to go on a walk and get very muddy
When we get home she has a nice warm bubble
bath
Which can be a laugh
Because all of a sudden there's a big loud splash!
My pet dog is my friend
She loves to give cuddles that you never want to
end.

Alfie Pheasey (9)

Wilbraham Primary School, Fallowfield

My Amazing Pet

My pet comes for cake
Even though it can't bake.
My pet is a superhero
And it doesn't like the number zero.
My pet saves humans
And its name is Buman.
I love my pet
And I never regret
Having a pet.

Zainab Muhumad (8)
Wilbraham Primary School, Fallowfield

My Pet Cat

My pet cat is strange like a rat.
My pet cat can fly like a bat.
My pet cat is furry like a mat.
My pet cat is the best cat in the world.

Sophia Rashid (8)
Wilbraham Primary School, Fallowfield

Look! There's A Cat!

Look! There's a cat!
Is it a cat chasing a rat?
Maybe looking for a hat?
No. It wants to have a chat!
"Hello, Mr Kitty Cat!"

Aqsa (11)
Wilbraham Primary School, Fallowfield

Child Of Shadows

Handsome, glorious, sacrificing self for renewal,
Building himself a pyre and setting himself ablaze.
For the sake of self, a red bird he becomes
And then comes forth through the ashes as a new
black and purple bird,
Shedding the old self off as it is no longer useful.
You embrace your new strengths and fly high into
the garden and up to the sun.
He will stay with me for as long as I live, for he is
immortal and I am not!
He embraces himself for he is the child of the
shadows and will live eternal, through birth, death
and renewal!
His spirit will live on for eternity!

Resa Amin (11)
Wyndcliffe Primary School, Birmingham

Max

My peculiar pet is Max,
I would never want to change,
For, although he may be different but
For me, he is always the same.

With a neck so long and wings to fly
Max will save the day.

From far or near he sees the danger and will
Be on his way.
No trouble is too big, no trouble is too small.
For Max, it's no problem at all.

He's friendly, kind and as sweet as can be.
Max is one in a million
And he is always there for me.

Eiliyah Bibi
Wyndcliffe Primary School, Birmingham

My Rockstar Puppy

R eady as I will always be,

O n my adventure, I go.

C alling all my friends,

K icking and rocking

S ongs as we explore.

T he life of a rockstar

A ltogether we unite,

R ocking our beauty,

P laying our music,

U ntil we stand.

P artying with our fans,

P articipating in fun with

Y ou and me!

Sakeenah Zafar

Wyndcliffe Primary School, Birmingham

Dragurtle

Dragurtle is the best!
Whenever I am in battle
I put on his saddle
He vanquishes my foes
Even though he is a bit slow
He has eight pointy claws
That are as sharp as saws!
I jump on his back and we go
High, high and higher
When we reach the battleground
He breathes a bit too much fire!

Those who dare
Disturb our lair
But they don't come back
Do you want to find out why?
Nobody can beat he and I
For...
Dragurtle is the best!

Idrees
Wyndcliffe Primary School, Birmingham

Emma The Electrical Eagle

My pet is the most peculiar of pets
She can be annoying but her purchase I do not regret
She gets up to a lot of mischief
But in my time of need, she is a relief

Emma is gifted with electrifying powers
She soars higher than the tallest of towers
Even though she can be a pain in the butt
If she is ever in danger, I'll take a punch to the gut.

Yaquub Musse Abdi (11)
Wyndcliffe Primary School, Birmingham

Tech-Savvy Puppy

This puppy is like no other,
It has no sister or brother.
Devices are all it knows.
If you are a tech-savvy puppy,
That's how it goes.
"I have many nicknames,
Sometimes I go as the tech-savvy puppy who plays games."

Anaya Kayani (8)
Wyndcliffe Primary School, Birmingham

My Terrific Tortoise

My terrific tortoise is the best you can find,
He can fly very high in the sky.
His name is Flash
And he can run as fast as a load of cats.
He is a brainy little guy, that you will want to buy!
He is sweet and sometimes sour,
He loves to hide in the shower.
You will love him, don't you see?
And he's all mine all for me.
You will also find him behind the sofa
Looking for crumbs and any leftovers.
Always getting up to mischief.
Always following me to the kitchen.
He's always next to me,
But I want him to be.
I love him very much.
I'm not making a fuss!
He has beautiful wings
And other magical things!

Lola McCarthy (9)
Ysgol Nantgwyn, Penygraig

The Butterfly That Didn't Fly

I am a butterfly, but did you know that I can't fly?
When I flap my wings very high, all I want to do is cry!

I try so hard not to give up
I fly across the yard, but I can't go up!

I sit upon a pretty flower and it gives me time to think.
I pray that one day I'll get the power, that I'll no longer sink!

One windy stormy day,
The wind lifts me away.
This is my day!
I learn to fly away!

I am now a butterfly,
I can fly up and up!
I am no longer scared to fly.
Remember to never give up!

Seren Carpenter (10)
Ysgol Nantgwyn, Penygraig

Magnificent Mac

M y dog is a magician
A nd he's very very good!
G reatness is a thing of his
N o one else even comes close!
I n the night he performs on stage,
F ascinating tricks he makes!
I n the blink of an eye
C oming out of his sleeve is a snake!
E verybody loves him!
N o one more than me.
T he best friend I could ever have.

M ac the magnificent...
A nd very furry
C lever little dog.

Jaiden Gregory (9)
Ysgol Nantgwyn, Penygraig

Fluffy The Bunny

Fluffy the bunny is not very funny,
His orange and black hair is enough to give you a scare!
He may look classy but he is actually quite sassy!
Rabbits are gentle and mild, but this one is dangerous and wild!
Don't be fooled by his cute looks, he is smarter than a dictionary book!
His teeth are sharp and his eyes are as black as the night.
He would even give a war hero a fright!
Although Fluffy would probably eat a bird or a dove, he is still the pet that I love.

Cole Jenkins (10)
Ysgol Nantgwyn, Penygraig

Eli The Exotic Elephant

Eli liked to dance about
Up and down, left and right
Eli's friends would all shout out
"Go to bed, it's late at night."

Eli was no ordinary elephant
He wore his shoes on the wrong feet.
And even though his friends would rant
He ignored them all and danced to the beat.

Another thing they all found strange
Was Eli wore a football kit.
One thing for sure they wouldn't change
Is Eli's dancing kept him fit.

Dafydd Gubbings (10)
Ysgol Nantgwyn, Penygraig

Didi The Speed Sloth

My name is Didi.
Although I'm a sloth I'm super speedy.
I'm anything but lazy.
In fact, I'm a little bit crazy!
I like to play games and have fun
I can never be outrun.
My fur is a bright colour green
So when I hide in trees I can't be seen.
When playing hide-and-seek I can never be found
I keep my friends looking all around.

Millie Phillps (9)
Ysgol Nantgwyn, Penygraig

The Big-Eared Giraffe

Once there was a big giraffe,
Who liked to have a little laugh.
He had big ears,
And not many fears.
With big, big claws to match.
Though he was very friendly,
Others thought he was very deadly.
Even though he was not,
They thought about it quite a lot.

Starr Morgan-Davies (9)
Ysgol Nantgwyn, Penygraig

Lola The Lovely Wolf

Lola is a lovely gentle wolf.
Never bites and never ever could.
She's tiny and wild and could never be tamed.
She's sassy and clever and no one outsmarts her.

Lynsey McCabe (10)
Ysgol Nantgwyn, Penygraig

The Spider Dog

S cared animal.

P erfect pet.

I t bites!

D on't come near!

E ats everything!

R eally scary!

Jake Green

Ysgol Nantgwyn, Penygraig

YOUNG wRITERS INFORMATION

We hope you have enjoyed reading this book – and that you will continue to in the coming years.

If you're a young writer who enjoys reading and creative writing, or the parent of an enthusiastic poet or story writer, visit our website **www.youngwriters.co.uk/subscribe** to join the World of Young Writers and receive news, competitions, writing challenges, tips, articles and giveaways! There is lots to keep budding writers motivated to write!

If you would like to order further copies of this book, or any of our other titles, then please give us a call or order via your online account.

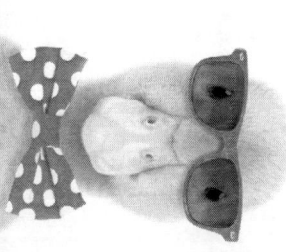

Young Writers
Remus House
Coltsfoot Drive
Peterborough
PE2 9BF
(01733) 890066
info@youngwriters.co.uk

Join in the conversation!
Tips, news, giveaways and much more!

 **YoungWritersUK**    **YoungWritersCW**    **youngwriterscw**